I SURRENDER ALL (SORT OF)

Laying Down Our Agendas
So God Can Do the Impossible

ENDORSEMENTS

Surrender is at the very core of the fruitful Christian life exemplified by Jesus's example of surrender to his Father's will. Because surrender is so significant, it may indeed be the most challenging part of our walk with Christ. Michelle S. Lazurek's book delves into that challenge with gracious encouragement found in hope from the Bible, humble vulnerability in her personal stories, and inspirational truths about God's desire to empower us. Surrender may be scary, but Michelle S. Lazurek's wisdom in *I Surrender All* meets you right where you live and leads you to joyful assurance that God's way is the best way.

—**Kathy Collard Miller**, International speaker and award-winning author of over 55 books including *God's Intriguing Questions: 60 New Testament Devotions Revealing Jesus's Nature.*

In *I Surrender All*, author Michelle S. Lazurek has provided us with a treasure of great worth. Her insight and biblical foundation give us a roadmap to walk closer with God through the exercise of surrender. This book provides transparent examples from her own life as well as practical tips to guide us through the process. This is a book to cherish and a book to give to those you love.

—**Edie Melson**, Award-winning author and director of the Blue Ridge Mountains Christian Writers Conference

Although the world shoves us toward haughty independence, this book is a lovely reminder that our true freedom is only found through dependence on God. Author Michelle S. Lazurek uses fresh biblical insights combined with modern-day anecdotes to drive home spiritual points that do indeed help us echo the beloved title, *I Surrender All*. The "Surrender Your Weapon" section was especially meaningful to me (and I suspect it will be to you, too!) in this strange, fierce, post-pandemic age that has forced many of us to brandish weapons of defense against personalized spiritual, emotional, and political assaults. Only when we lower our weapons do we find that the answer to a joy-filled, peace-filled, Jesus-filled life is surrender. I highly recommend this book!"

—**Debora M. Coty**, Award-winning author of over 30 inspirational books, including the best-selling *Too Blessed to be Stressed* series

In a world that applauds when we go, go, go, or do, do, do, or be, be, be, it can be difficult to surrender all that we do, think, feel, or are. Not only do others place expectations on us, but we place high expectations on ourselves, often leaving us tired, worn, and weary. Too often we try to make things happen in our own effort and strength. *I Surrender All* reorients the reader's perspective away from an independent, works-driven life to one fully dependent on God through sacrifice, hard work, and a determination to let God be God in our lives.

—**Dr. Michelle Bengtson,** Podcast host and author of the multi-award-winning *Hope Prevails: Insights from a Doctor's Personal Journey Through Depression* and *Breaking Anxiety's Grip: How to Reclaim the Peace God Promises*

I Surrender All (Sort Of) opens the door to the freedom for which we all frenetically hunt but cannot seem to find. Michelle authentically shares the difficulty with surrender, her own brave battle to embrace it, and the beautiful result it brought into her life. This book is a must read when waiting, feeling restless, or struggling with discontent.

—**Erica Wiggenhorn**, Author of *Letting God Be Enough: Why Striving Keeps You Stuck and How Surrender Sets You Free* from Moody Publishers.

I SURRENDER ALL (SORT OF)

Laying Down Our Agendas So God Can Do the Impossible

Michelle S. Lazurek

Copyright Notice

I Surrender All (Sort Of): Laying Down Our Agendas So God Can Do the Impossible

First edition. Copyright © 2022 by Michelle S. Lazurek. The information contained in this book is the intellectual property of Michelle S. Lazurek and is governed by United States and International copyright laws. All rights reserved. No part of this publication, either text or image, may be used for any purpose other than personal use. Therefore, reproduction, modification, storage in a retrieval system, or retransmission, in any form or by any means, electronic, mechanical, or otherwise, for reasons other than personal use, except for brief quotations for reviews or articles and promotions, is strictly prohibited without prior written permission by the publisher.

All Scripture quotations, unless otherwise indicated, are taken from the Holy Bible, New International Version®, NIV®. Copyright ©1973, 1978, 1984, 2011 by Biblica, Inc.™ Used by permission of Zondervan. All rights reserved worldwide. www.zondervan.com The "NIV" and "New International Version" are trademarks registered in the United States Patent and Trademark Office by Biblica, Inc.™

Scriptures labeled ESV are taken from *The Holy Bible, English Standard Version.* Copyright ©2000, 2001 by Crossway Bibles, a division of Good News Publishers. Used by permission. All rights reserved.

Cover and Interior Design: Derinda Babcock
Editor(s): Cheri Fields, Deb Haggerty

Author Represented By: WordWise Media Services

PUBLISHED BY: Elk Lake Publishing, Inc., 35 Dogwood Drive, Plymouth, MA 02360, 2022

Library Cataloging Data

Names: Lazurek, Michelle (Michelle Lazurek)

I Surrender All (Sort Of): Laying Down Our Agendas So God Can Do the Impossible / Michelle S. Lazurek

170 p. 23cm × 15cm (9in × 6 in.)

ISBN-13: 978-1-64949-401-6 (paperback) | 978-1-64949-400-9 (trade paperback) | 978-1-64949-399-6 (e-book)

Key Words: God's presence, intimacy with God, awe, devotional, inspirational, going deeper with God, everyday miracles

Library of Congress Control Number: 2022933665

TO JOE

Thanks for walking this journey of surrender with me.

CONTENTS

To Joe ix
Acknowledgments xi
Introduction 1
Surrender Your Weapons 7
Surrender Your Expectations. 13
Surrender Your Promised Land 21
Surrender Your Fears 29
Surrender Your Disappointments 39
Chapter Six—Surrender Your Doubts 45
Chapter Seven—Surrender Your To-Do Lists. 49
Chapter Eight—Surrender Your Will 55
Chapter Nine—Surrender Your Pride. 63
Chapter Ten—Surrender Your Devotions. 73
Chapter Eleven—Surrender Your Identity 85
Chapter Twelve—Surrender Your Vision 95
Chapter Thirteen—Surrender Your Disagreements 101
Chapter Fourteen—Surrender Your Marriage 113
Chapter Fifteen—Surrender Your Children's
Identities 121

Chapter Sixteen—Surrender Your Finances 127

Chapter Seventeen—Surrender Your Work 137

Chapter Eighteen—Surrender Your Possessions. . . 145

Chapter Nineteen—Live a Surrendered Life 151

Endnotes 153

Additional Resources 155

About the Author 157

ACKNOWLEDGMENTS

Although every book I write is personal, this one is the most personal. It is never easy to talk about struggles with mental health, but my hope is that by talking about it in an honest way like this, it will remove the stigma mental health still has in society, especially the church. If you struggle with mental health, make discussing it openly with the people around you a priority, so they have a better understanding of the journey surrounding mental health.

With every book I write, I can't help but reflect on the many people who had a hand, whether directly or indirectly, in the production of this book. If it were not for the support of the following people, this book would not be possible:

To Susan Lower, Edie Melson, Kathy Carlton Willis, and the faculty at the St. David's Christian Writers Conference. On one ordinary day in 2018, I enlisted the help of two writer friends, and together, we fleshed out the outline for this book. They encouraged me to pursue this and said every Christian needs to learn how to surrender. It is through their encouragement and through Susan and her faculty's perseverance that this book is now in print. This is one of many reasons why writing is not to be done in isolation, but in community.

To my agent Steve Hutson for believing in my work, and more importantly, me. Thanks for not only taking me on as a client but also as a colleague.

To Deb Haggerty, Derinda Babcock, and Cheri Fields for your tireless work on this book. Even in the moments when I have wanted to quit, your belief in this project has been the impetus to keep me going. For every author to whom you give a voice, I'm convinced your heavenly rewards increase exponentially.

To the members of Locust Valley Chapel, Nate and Sharon Howard, Paul Bauer, and Rebekah Sampson, thank you for your gracious acceptance of me during my trials with anxiety. Your cards, gifts, and support mean more than you know. You have demonstrated being the hands and feet of Christ in tangible ways.

To Joe, Caleb and Leah, no matter how many awards I win or books I write, you are three of the best rewards I have ever received. Thank you for loving me through this journey.

As always, thank you, Jesus, for your presence in my life, your miraculous intervention, and the gift of your death on the cross. I may never fully understand the depths of your love for me on earth but thank you for choosing me to do the work of the kingdom.

INTRODUCTION

Hustle.
    Prepare.
        Become.
            Wash.
                Be.

As I skimmed my hands across the book spines poking out from the shelves of my local bookstore, these were some of the words in the titles. I'm a type A, driven person—they spoke to my perfectionistic heart. The thought that I could have the spiritual life I longed for simply by doing more made my heart leap. After all, who doesn't love the thought of taking their life out of God's hands and into their own?

Then my heart sank.

The past year had been difficult for me. As someone who jumps at the chance to use my writing ability for God's glory, I had been in what I would call a holding pattern with God. For years, God had revealed writing project after writing project to me, much to my delight, and as someone who is happiest when she is checking items off her to-do list, this season of waiting frustrated me more than anything. No matter how hard I asked (OK, begged) God to reveal his future for me as a writer, I heard nothing but radio static.

On top of this, my financial health was deteriorating at an alarming rate. Car repairs mounted, school outings required more than my wallet held, and my bank account dwindled into the negative numbers. As my finances went down, my stress levels went up and so did the number on my bathroom scale. In just a matter of weeks, my life was crumbling around me, and there was nothing I could do about it.

Little did I know, I was in the best position in my life.

Surrender, according to Merriam-Webster's dictionary means to "cease resistance to an enemy or opponent and submit to their authority; give in, give (oneself) up."[1] Not only does surrender mean to lay down the things that mean the most to us, but it also means to submit to someone else's authority, giving them full control over our lives.

A synonym for surrender is "capitulate" which means to "cease to resist an opponent or an unwelcome demand."[2] Not only does surrender mean to give up my stuff, but it also means to give up my tendency to wrestle with God trying to manipulate him into giving me the answer I desire.

Surrender means I say, "I'm not the boss. But you are, God."

Can I be honest?

Surrender stinks.

Surrender means I no longer have the final word.

Surrender means I'm no longer in charge.

In my case, what God was asking of me was not to do more but quite the opposite. He was asking me to stop trying to fix things myself and allow him to do a miraculous work. It wasn't until I laid down my weapon of control and everything else that separated me from a dependent relationship with God that I allowed God to transform me.

Maybe the answer to increasing my intimacy with God is not doing more but doing less.

Was this really the answer to the joy-filled life I had been looking for?

I SURRENDER ALL (SORT OF) | 3

In the middle of worship team practice a few years ago, my friend Steve burst out, "Why do we call it 'I Surrender All?' We only surrender some."

Perplexed, I asked him what he meant.

"Well, we sing about how we surrender all, but that's not quite true. We only surrender part of our lives, not all our lives to God. I mean, at least that's what I do."

I didn't give any thought to what he had said until I had time to ponder it later. How often do we consider the meaning behind the words we sing? We sing and raise our hands in worship on Sunday, but how do we live the other six days of the week when we don't connect with him?

If I'm honest, I surrender some of my life, but do I really surrender all? Most of us desire to yield all our lives for God, but there's just that one—or two or three things—we just don't want to give up.

Not yet anyway.

When my husband was a little boy, he enjoyed playing cards with his grandfather. He loved to play Rummy 500, where a player picks up one card on their turn and discards one onto the discard pile. If a player wants a card in the discard pile to create their three cards of the same suit, they can pick up that card, but they must also pick up all the cards beneath it (if there are any). Once a player gets three cards in a row, either of the same number or in the same suit, he can put those cards down, reducing the number in his hand.

Often his grandfather would pick up all the cards in the discard pile, only to lay down one set of three matching cards. When my husband asked him why he did that, he said, "The more you lay down, the more you can pick up." Hand after hand, his grandfather would pick up almost all the cards in the discard pile and round after round lay them down in acceptable matches to win the game. This seemed counterintuitive to my husband. Wouldn't it make more sense to pick up fewer, so he could control the outcome and lay down fewer matches? How could picking up more result in winning a card game?

Because his grandfather didn't win because of what he *picked up,* he won because of what he *laid down.* But still holding cards when his grandfather discarded the last card in his hand would have led to his loss. When he chose to lay down the things that ensured his win (his matching cards) he ensured his success.

Jesus is not a distant God waiting for us to mess up our lives. Jesus wants us all to thrive. But he also wants us to cry out to him when we have failed. First John 3 wants us to be reminded of who we truly are in Christ: "See what great love the Father has lavished on us, that we should be called children of God! And that is what we are! The reason the world does not know us is that it did not know him."

Throughout this book, I will ask you to lay down whatever it is that is keeping you from living a life of surrender. Then we will talk about what you can pick up to move forward in surrender. In some chapters, I'll suggest one thing to lay down and one thing to pick up. In some chapters, surrender will require laying down and picking up more than one thing. We will also wrestle with the paradox that surrender doesn't mean doing nothing but may mean doing the right thing. It means renewing our minds about concepts we thought we knew, then reapplying new concepts to our everyday lives. I don't just want this to be a quick read that you place on the bookshelf and never apply. My goal is for this book to be a resource of practical strategies that you can apply today to experience the freedom that dependence on God can give to your life.

My prayer for you as you read this book is to learn what it means to truly surrender. As we learn to lay down our lives in surrender and God begins to fill every area of our lives, our actions change. Once we are filled with the Spirit and not ourselves, we can freely pass on this gift of surrender to others. My hope is you pass on what you learn in this book to others. If you are like me, you will find it won't be easy. Everything in you will want to resist because *doing something* rather than laying down your life will feel like you are still in control. In the same way Jesus pled for an escape from his upcoming crucifixion but surrendered his life to his Father's will on the cross, you will learn what it means to surrender every facet of your life—your expectations, your will, your pride.

—1—
SURRENDER YOUR WEAPONS

In Exodus 14:5–14, the Israelites were asked to lay down the things that ensured their success.

> As Pharaoh approached, the Israelites looked up, and there were the Egyptians, marching after them. They were terrified and cried out to the LORD. They said to Moses, "Was it because there were no graves in Egypt that you brought us to the desert to die? What have you done to us by bringing us out of Egypt? Didn't we say to you in Egypt, 'Leave us alone; let us serve the Egyptians'? It would have been better for us to serve the Egyptians than to die in the desert!" Moses answered the people, "Do not be afraid. Stand firm and you will see the deliverance the LORD will bring you today. The Egyptians you see today you will never see again. The LORD will fight for you; you need only to be still."

The Israelites were looking at the huge army encroaching upon them. Greatly outnumbered, they were terrified they would be defeated. The Israelites cried out in terror to God. In response to their cries, Moses replies, "Be still."

Be still? What kind of military strategy is that? How could they possibly win the war by laying down their weapons? Talk about counterintuitive!

By laying down their weapons, they made themselves

totally vulnerable. They had to trade in their independence—their ability to fight the war on their own—for dependence on God. But it was only when they yielded their lives and safety to him that God could move on their behalf, and God moved mightily. The rest of Exodus describes what he did amid the Israelites after they made the conscious choice to lay down their weapons, be still, and let the Lord fight for them.

The story in Exodus continues to demonstrate God's miraculous work and presence:

> Then the LORD said to Moses, "Why are you crying out to me? Tell the Israelites to move on. Raise your staff and stretch out your hand over the sea to divide the water so that the Israelites can go through the sea on dry ground. I will harden the hearts of the Egyptians so that they will go in after them. And I will gain glory through Pharaoh and all his army, through his chariots and his horsemen. The Egyptians will know that I am the LORD when I gain glory through Pharaoh, his chariots and his horsemen." Then the angel of God, who had been traveling in front of Israel's army, withdrew and went behind them. The pillar of cloud also moved from in front and stood behind them coming between the armies of Egypt and Israel. Throughout the night the cloud brought darkness to the one side and light to the other side; so neither went near the other all night long. Then Moses stretched out his hand over the sea, and all that night the LORD drove the sea back with a strong east wind and turned it into dry land. The waters were divided, and the Israelites went through the sea on dry ground, with a wall of water on their right and on their left. (Exodus 14:15–22)

Look at all God did once the Israelites leaned on him and not themselves. As Christians, we often choose to walk our spiritual walk without other brothers and sisters in Christ, watching the latest sermon online or listening to the latest podcast without regular church attendance or gathering in a group. But it is only when we choose to fight our battles together, to lay down our weapons, that God can do what only he can do.

It's not just in the Old Testament God asks this of his people. Luke 9:1–6 describes Jesus's plan for sending out the disciples to spread the gospel message:

> When Jesus had called the Twelve together, he gave them power and authority to drive out all demons and to cure diseases, and he sent them out to proclaim the kingdom of God and to heal the sick. He told them: "Take nothing for the journey—no staff, no bag, no bread, no money, no extra shirt. Whatever house you enter, stay there until you leave that town. If people do not welcome you, leave their town and shake the dust off your feet as a testimony against them." So they set out and went from village to village, proclaiming the good news and healing people everywhere.

Jesus requires his disciples not to rely on themselves when they minister to their communities. Whether it's missionaries who rely on their local church for support or a church that takes a love offering for a family in need, God wants his people to rely on him for all their provisions—from shelter to clothing—so they can better understand what it was like for Jesus to walk the earth. He wanted the disciples to live lives of dependence rather than independence. To be a follower of Christ means to strip yourself of everything you have that makes you rely on yourself rather than on God.

As they went out on Jesus's mission, the disciples were in the best position of their lives—and yet the most vulnerable at the same time.

It was much like that in my life, too. As much as I wanted to work, hustle, strive, to control the results in my life, even more, God wanted me to lay them down.

Lay down my weight.

Lay down my finances.

Lay down my work.

Lay down my independence.

What keeps you from surrendering your weapons? Maybe your weapon is unforgiveness, which you wield at loved ones and other people who have hurt you. Perhaps your weapon is your lack of trust in God. Circumstances have hurt you so much you fear that, if you become fully dependent on God, you risk hurt, pain and disappointment.

Whatever your weapon of choice is, it's keeping you from living a life of surrender. A life so yielded to God he gets to lead the way in everything, allowing him full access to every nook and cranny of your heart.

It's scary, I know. Trust me, I'm there with you.

Picking Up Peace

But when the Israelites laid down their weapons, they picked up peace during a life-threatening situation. When the disciples laid down their comfort and independence, they picked up provision from other brothers and sisters in Christ—to the glory of God.

When I lay down my independence, I get to hold the hand of my Abba Father and trust he will lead me into a more intimate relationship with him.

And when I lay down my weapons, I win the war every time.

LAYING IT DOWN

1. Why do you think God asks us to be still before he will move in our lives?

2. What weapon(s) do you need to lay down to have a dependent relationship with God?

3. How do you live a life of independence?

4. How do you think society encourages us to live independent lives?

—2—
SURRENDER YOUR EXPECTATIONS

If I want to begin to live a life of surrender, I have to start with my expectations, because we too often have our own ideas of what success will look like. But God may have different ideas about that. If we don't open ourselves fully to God, we may miss out on his perfect plan for us. Peter is a great example of having to surrender what he believed success would look like to fulfill God's purposes for his life. Matthew 14:26–30 speaks about Peter's obedience—and ultimate surrender of his safety—to fulfill Jesus's calling:

> When the disciples saw him walking on the lake, they were terrified. "It's a ghost," they said, and cried out in fear. But Jesus immediately said to them: "Take courage! It is I. Don't be afraid." "Lord, if it's you," Peter replied, "tell me to come to you on the water." "Come," he said. Then Peter got down out of the boat, walked on the water and came toward Jesus. But when he saw the wind, he was afraid and, beginning to sink, cried out, "Lord, save me!"

When Peter called out to Jesus, Jesus said, "Come." Peter must have thought he would immediately be a success at walking on water. After all, he had sat under Jesus's teaching for several years. But Peter still needed Jesus's reassurance that it was truly him asking him to come out onto the water.

Maybe Peter's insecurity or doubt kept him from immediate obedience, but whatever it was, Peter needed to recognize Jesus's voice to take that step of faith.

Sometimes we need to lay down our preconceived notions and yield them to learn from an expert in their field of expertise. For example, as a writer, I learned a lot of what I know about writing on my own, but I had a great mentor in the beginning of my writing journey. When my children were young, their preschool teacher was also a writer. I asked her if she would guide me in my journey as a writer, and she agreed. For months after that request, we went to critique groups together, bringing samples of our work to the group to have them slice and dice our work. It often felt as if they were surgeons who cut open a cadaver to practice surgical procedures. It wasn't easy to have my hard work opened up for criticism, but it made me a better writer—and ultimately, a better person in the long run.

Writing was not what I imagined it to be. I believed, like Ralphie in the movie *A Christmas Story*, every publisher was going to love my work, then hoist me on their shoulders and parade me around as their next best thing in writing. But as we know, that's a nice idea, but not rooted in reality.

Peter probably expected the same thing. He probably expected planting both feet firmly on the water and walking with confidence toward Jesus. After all, he had learned from Jesus himself for a while now and assumed he could simply emulate what he saw. For a few steps, he was doing great, but all too soon he faltered and ended in failure. Similarly, I, like Peter, expected to simply write great stories, and they would be perfect the first time, every time. But that simply was not the case. If I was going to get better at honing my craft, I'd need to surrender my expectations of how easy writing would be, and humble myself, assuming a posture of teachability.

Lay Down Your Expectations

To have an expectation means you want a situation to go a certain way. It is a form of control, and unchecked can threaten others' emotional security. In Matthew 16:21–27, Jesus lays out his expectations for his disciples:

> Then Jesus said to his disciples, "Whoever wants to be my disciple must deny themselves and take up their cross and follow me. For whoever wants to save their life will lose it, but whoever loses their life for me will find it. What good will it be for someone to gain the whole world, yet forfeit their soul? Or what can anyone give in exchange for their soul? For the Son of Man is going to come in his Father's glory with his angels, and then he will reward each person according to what they have done."

What an expectation! The disciples believed life would be easy with Jesus. What a cost to follow him—to deny themselves and endure whatever persecution came their way! Can you imagine what the disciples were thinking when Jesus said this? He expected them to give up every aspect of themselves—including their lives—to be his follower. Jesus then blindsides them with the prophetic truth that Peter is actually a stumbling block to his ministry. Jesus was always asking them to lay down their expectations and trade them for a life of surprise with him.

The disciples had it tough from the start. Matthew 4:18–22 says,

> As Jesus was walking beside the Sea of Galilee, he saw two brothers, Simon called Peter and his brother Andrew. They were casting a net into the lake, for they were fishermen. "Come, follow me," Jesus said, "and I will send you out to fish for people." At once they left their nets and followed him. Going on from there, he saw two other brothers, James son of Zebedee and his brother John. They were in a boat

with their father Zebedee, preparing their nets. Jesus called them, and immediately they left the boat and their father and followed him.

With these two words, "follow me," the Lord is asking them to lay down everything and trust that his life is better than the life they were used to. A fisherman's life, although not the most lucrative, was still a guarantee of regular income at a trade they learned from their ancestors. When the Lord asks them to lay down their life, he is asking them to lay down their notions of what a successful, fulfilling life will look like.

Jesus does the same with us. In this world, nothing is stable. It was the same for the disciples whom Jesus asked to simply follow him with no promise of where they were going, what would result, or even if they would be successful at it. John got to live to an old age, even writing Revelation because of the visions God gave him. Yet Peter was martyred for the faith.

When we look at Jesus's life, some people might perceive Jesus as a failure. At the end of his life, no disciples were courageous enough to stay with him except for John; few of the people whom he healed or drove demons out of even dared show up to his crucifixion! Yet, he had spent three straight years healing, caring, and preaching to the masses.

PICK UP TRUE SUCCESS

When we experience what we perceive as failure, we want to quit and root our identity in performance rather than in who we are as God's children. It is easy to believe that when you fail, God can't use you in ministry. But just when things seem like they are over, and you can't fail anymore, God reorients, and sometimes redirects, us to a new ministry or chapter in life.

Sometimes we don't truly know who God is. We get glimpses of who he is, and we make connections based on our experiences and what little we know of him in the Word of God.

This is why it is important to redefine our failures. Yes, we will fail in life. But when we stop defining our success by the world's standards and start defining it by taking those steps toward God, we can cry out to God in a vulnerable moment of weakness and simply be children who need their daddies to pick them up when they fall and help them get back into the boat.

> But he said to me, "My grace is sufficient for you, for my power is made perfect in weakness." Therefore, I will boast all the more gladly of my weaknesses, so that the power of Christ may rest upon me. For the sake of Christ, then, I am content with weaknesses, insults, hardships, persecutions, and calamities. For when I am weak, then I am strong. (Second Corinthians 12:9–10)

God reveals his power in and through us when we fail. Although failure is hard to deal with at the time, it is an opportunity to experience God's power in our lives, because he demonstrates how strong he is in our moments of weakness.

When our identities are rooted and built up in being children of God and heirs to the throne, then we can feel free to fail and understand that it is not the end of our story. We can get back up when we have fallen and know it is simply the end of a chapter, not the end of the story.

Pick Up Confidence

The American Dream encourages independence and a performance-based work ethic to achieve success. Yet, by Jesus's example, this is not his dream for us. All that hard work can get you ahead in the world, but what if none of that work matters to God? What a horrible life to lead!

Ginny Dent Brant shared a personal testimony with me of how her father had expectations for her career and direction in life:

> I felt God calling me to learn his Word and to help others. I was a successful model at the time. I surrendered my modeling career, but when God led me to leave the university, I was to transfer to a Bible college to get my biblical education, my father was not happy about my direction in training or career. He paid for my brother to attend Harvard, and for my sister and brother to attend well-recognized schools, but he refused to pay for me to go to such a place. I surrendered to God's will for my life and worked my way through school. It was painful to not have his approval and support. I felt torn between my earthly father and my heavenly father.
>
> As my father saw the changes in me and what I was willing to do and give up following God's calling on my life, he eventually did the same. He gave up his political career to go into full-time ministry, attended that Bible college at age fifty to get his biblical foundation, and God led him to Romania where he planted fifty churches after the communist walls fell, and he helped the country and underground churches to come to freedom.[1]

If life is merely a vapor, then we should make the most of it today. Jesus said, "Therefore I tell you, do not worry about your life, what you will eat or drink; or about your body, what you will wear. Is not life more than food, and the body more than clothes? Look at the birds of the air; they do not sow or reap or store away in barns, and yet your heavenly Father feeds them. Are you not much more valuable than they? Can any one of you by worrying add a single hour to your life?" (Matthew 6:25–27). Instead of controlling every event in our lives, let's live a life confident in who we are, and that God has our best in mind.

Children are confident in how they approach life. They expect adults will care for their every need and are not afraid to speak their minds and ask for what they want, no matter how outlandish it might be. God wants us to approach him with the boldness of a child, like in Matthew 7:9–11: "Which of you, if your son asks for bread, will give him a stone? Or if he asks for a fish, will give him a snake? If you, then, though you are evil, know how to give good gifts to your children, how much more will your Father in heaven give good gifts to those who ask him!"

To live a life of confidence means I have to surrender total control of a situation so I can allow God to work. God invites us to first yield our lives to him, bowing to his will and allowing him to speak into our lives, and then to boldly come to him for everything we need.

LAYING IT DOWN

1. How do your current expectations about your life affect how you see the world?

2. In what ways do you approach God with boldness like a child?

3. If you have difficulty approaching God with your requests, what's one thing you can do to change that?

—3—
SURRENDER YOUR PROMISED LAND

"I think God's calling me to plant a church."

These were my husband's words to me one random day a year after accepting our first pastoral position as newlyweds. Two years later, God called us to move back to our hometown to plant a church.

In theory, it sounded great. All it would require was a long drive back home to Connecticut to gather a group of committed Christians looking to make a difference in our town, and God would take it from there. In theory. Fast forward four years after he sensed our initial calling to plant a church: I worked at a daycare to keep a roof over our heads while my husband took a job as an associate pastor at a church within our district (which he never would have taken unless God used the job to lead him home), all the while not finding any people from that church wanting to plant with us. This left my husband and me scratching our heads and wondering if we had heard from God at all.

This was far from our promised land.

Finally, five years later, we opened the doors of a Knights of Columbus hall to hold a public worship service for our church plant, called Praxis Church because of our goal to "put instruction into action." We wanted to help Christians apply the Bible they knew in their minds and allow it to pierce (and ultimately transform) their lives. With only twelve adults from our home church committed to joining the journey with us, it was far from an easy road. But surely the Lord would give us success because of our obedience, right?

Wrong.

Dozens of people flitted in and out of our services over those first few months. Then my husband received a call from the owner of the building where we were meeting saying that the archdiocese didn't want us to meet in their predominantly Catholic hall and wanted us to leave immediately. Packing up our things, we found another hall in a nearby town, which had been rented to partygoers the night before. Sundays often began with picking up drug-infused needles in the parking lot and cleaning up debris on the hall's sticky, hardwood floor.

Every Sunday service in that hall something went wrong. Sometimes our worship music competed with the hollers and screams of the couple fighting in the apartment next door. Soon we moved again, only to find the owner of the building violated fire codes by having our group of now thirty people meet there without a properly marked emergency exit. A year later, we moved again. And again.

After five and a half years of keeping the church afloat, six locations, dozens of people who came for a time only to leave again, and several pay cuts later, we were financially, emotionally, and physically exhausted. Honestly, I felt duped.

After yet another financial blow, we weren't making enough money to keep our own home, let alone pay rent at the church, and were already saddled with a mountain of debt for years. We knew it was time to close the doors. Beaten up spiritually, my husband took a pastorate in

I SURRENDER ALL (SORT OF) | 23

Pennsylvania, which meant another move for our family.

As we packed our belongings and headed for our parsonage in Pennsylvania, one thought ran through our heads. Where was our promised land?

Numbers 14:7–8 tells us what the promised land looked like: "The land we passed through and explored is exceedingly good. If the LORD is pleased with us, he will lead us into that land, a land flowing with milk and honey, and will give it to us. Only do not rebel against the LORD."

According to these verses, God said he would send the Israelites to the promised land, a place flowing with wonderful things, if he was pleased with them.

Wasn't God pleased with us?

Doesn't every one of his children whom God is pleased with deserve their own promised land?

Apparently, God's plan was not to deliver us into our promised land. Eventually, I made peace with that. But not without years of grief and confusion.

And we weren't the only ones who never saw their promised land.

Hebrews 11:1–4 and 13 describe those who in faith completed the callings God had placed on their lives:

> Now faith is confidence in what we hope for and assurance about what we do not see. This is what the ancients were commended for. By faith we understand that the universe was formed at God's command, so that what is seen was not made out of what was visible. By faith Abel brought God a better offering than Cain did. By faith he was commended as righteous, when God spoke well of his offerings. And by faith Abel still speaks, even though he is dead. By faith Enoch was taken from this life, so that he did not experience death: "He could not be found, because God had taken him away." For before he was taken, he was commended as one who pleased God. And without faith it is impossible to please God, because

anyone who comes to him must believe that he exists and that he rewards those who earnestly seek him...
They did not receive the things promised; they only saw them and welcomed them from a distance..."

I don't know why God gives earthly rewards to some people and not to others. In fact, it can seem downright unfair when I wait months for a financial upswing only to see a neighbor receive another promotion. I wish I could tell you I am never frustrated by this. I wish I could tell you I take all this waiting in stride because of my close, intimate relationship with my Father, who I believe gives me good gifts in his timing.

But the truth is I want my milk and honey, and I want it now.

I often forget to rely on my heavenly Father to give good gifts or divide inheritances evenly. I easily slip into wanting whatever everyone else is getting and then some. Like Sally says to Charlie Brown, "I just want what's coming to me. I just want my fair share."

If I have dedicated my life to the mission of God, shouldn't he give me my just desserts?

A part of me wants to celebrate and be honored in front of everyone I know and be seen as special, wanted, loved. Like Ralphie in *A Christmas Story*, I want the teacher to write my name on the board with A++++ after it. I want my friends to hoist me on their shoulders and chant my name as I blow kisses to my adoring fans. But we all know that is just a movie. It's just a feeling, an ideal of what life should be. Sometimes my rewards are not seen this side of heaven.

Lay Down Your Rewards

In this life, I may never see the results of my work. My efforts to make disciples or do God's work may not be easily

I SURRENDER ALL (SORT OF) | 25

measured here on earth. I may never receive a tangible reward for the work I do during my lifetime. However, the more I yield myself to God's will for my life, the more opportunities he will give me to make more disciples.

Yet, I hope in this, "As the heavens are higher than the earth, so are my ways higher than your ways and my thoughts than your thoughts" (Psalm 55:6).

If I want to live a life of surrender, I have to swap out my hopes for a promised land and trade it for the satisfaction that comes from knowing success is not measured by numbers but by obedience.

I may never understand God's timeline for his children. I don't understand why some of his children, after all their work, are only allowed to see part of something great, while others get to reap the amazing benefits. For example, why do some pastors do the hard work of casting vision and empowering leaders, only to leave and have a second pastor reap the benefits of numeric and spiritual growth? If I want to live a life of surrender, I must give up my own idea of what a reasonable time frame is for my results versus what God has to say about—and how he defines—results. The amount of time we are given is not as important to God as what we do with that time. Hebrews 11:32–39 describes the results God looks for—and enables—through our obedience if we choose to give God our all:

> And what more shall I say? I do not have time to talk about Gideon, Barak, Samson and Jephthah, about David and Samuel and the prophets, who through faith conquered kingdoms, administered justice, and gained what was promised; who shut the mouths of lions, quenched the fury of the flames, and escaped the edge of the sword; whose weakness was turned to strength; and who became powerful in battle and routed foreign armies. Women received back their dead, raised to life again. There were others who were

tortured, refusing to be released so that they might gain an even better resurrection. Some faced jeers and flogging, and even chains and imprisonment. They were put to death by stoning; they were sawed in two; they were killed by the sword. They went about in sheepskins and goatskins, destitute, persecuted, and mistreated—the world was not worthy of them. They wandered in deserts and mountains, living in caves and in holes in the ground. These were all commended for their faith, yet none of them received what had been promised.

Pick Up Obedience

I can take solace in the fact that I, like Abel, gave God my very best offering and laid it at his feet. I, like Noah, consider it joy that plank by plank my husband and I built our ark (or planted our church) simply because he asked us to. I, like Abraham, can know that God may not choose to make my descendants on earth as numerous as the stars, but I have multiplied my impact on heaven, and that treasure will be stored there until I reach heaven.

Luke 19:13–19 reveals God's promise to reward those who invest their time and resources in others:

> So he called ten of his servants and gave them ten minas. "Put this money to work," he said, "until I come back." But his subjects hated him and sent a delegation after him to say, "We don't want this man to be our king." He was made king, however, and returned home. Then he sent for the servants to whom he had given the money, in order to find out what they had gained with it. The first one came and said, "Sir, your mina has earned ten more." "Well done, my good servant!" his master replied. "Because you have been trustworthy in a very small matter, take charge of ten cities." The second came and said, "Sir, your mina has earned five more." His master answered, "You take charge of five cities."

I choose to believe my obedience is what God finds commendable, even if there is no earthly promised land. I may not get what I think I deserve in this life, but I know every day I choose to obey God, I please him, and that itself is its own reward.

LAYING IT DOWN

1. What is your promised land? What is the earthly reward you thought God was going to give you for all your hard work in service to him?

2. Have you ever felt duped by God? Did you think God was going to reward you for your work, only to find out you never received what you hoped?

3. What steps can you take to surrender your promised land? How do you think you will grow spiritually if you can surrender it?

—4—
SURRENDER YOUR FEARS

I learned a part of surrender while staring at the bottom of an empty bottle of anti-anxiety medication.

Let me explain.

The year 2020 turned out to be hard for me, one of the hardest of my life. But while most of the world would say the same due to the pandemic, my world came crashing down *before* COVID-19 hit. Little did I know the coronavirus would be one of the greatest gifts to me.

I have always struggled with anxiety. As a kid, I came from a controlling home, with a mother who was usually quiet but often blew up at the smallest things. I walked on eggshells around her all the time, never knowing if I would say or do something that would make her mad. As a result, I had a constant sense of "butterflies in my stomach." Paired with a "children should be seen and not heard" unspoken rule that was a part of our family dynamic, I never knew what was going to happen. I learned to just be silent, unable to express myself well in many ways, particularly my feelings. This did not bode well for me as I grew into an adult. The anxiety I experienced as a child, I put in a box, locked away, and suppressed until I couldn't contain it anymore.

My panic attacks started in January of 2020. Financial woes, work-related tensions, and other factors caused me to start feeling anxious all the time. At first, my panic attacks occurred sporadically, lasting only a couple of minutes. But the more anxiety I experienced, the longer it took for the waves of panic to subside. I felt like an emergency button had been pushed in my gut, and I couldn't get it to stop.

Finally, I realized these were the same patterns in my adult life that I experienced in my childhood, so I reached out to a local counselor. He was good at giving me assignments as to how to forgive and move on from my past, but he couldn't stop the anxiety. Dr. Michelle Bengston, author of *Breaking Anxiety's Grip* says, "Anxiety frequently accompanies major life stressors, but for many, there is no obviously identifiable trigger. Anxiety often begins small and inconsequential, but left untreated, it often takes a life of its own and can become incapacitating."[1] I would soon find out that statement would become me.

The anxiety got so bad I stopped functioning normally. After the counselor recommended I see a psychologist, I knew I was at the end of myself. For weeks, I met with healthcare professionals and journaled my feelings. We tested different medications and monitored my progress, and I was finally diagnosed with generalized anxiety disorder. As I stared at the ceiling one night in my bed, thoughts raced through my head:

What is happening?

Is this really my life?

Who do I have to help me navigate through this tough season?

I learned a lot of techniques about how to deal with my anxiety. Instead of dwelling on my plight all day long, I learned mindfulness. This meant I could meditate on something good to break my train of thought from dwelling on bad thoughts for too long. I also learned how to use activities I enjoyed, like listening to music and taking a walk outside to allow myself a break from ominous thoughts and focus on music that gave me joy. I often hummed old '80s music or worship tunes in my head to remind myself it was all going to be OK.

I learned how relaxing activities like painting or coloring could be an outlet when the panic became too much to bear. I painted sailboats in pastel hues and placed them alongside the mirror on my bedroom dresser, an ever-present physical reminder that the most important work I was doing during this time was emotional healing. I recited positive affirmations to myself like, "It's OK not to know everything," and "Do the next right thing." This helped me take baby steps when my day became too overwhelming.

Perhaps the best technique I learned was to sort through boundaries and how to take each day one at a time. To create boundaries meant I needed to learn where to take responsibility for my mistakes and failures and where to allow others to deal with and accept their own issues. Soon I could navigate my panic attacks as they came, and the future didn't feel so overwhelming.

Then something happened.

My New Normal

I turned on the TV to see the governor of our state and other professionals urging people to stay home in what they called "quarantine." "This should only be for two weeks," my husband said. Our church's building shut down, and instead of attending in person, we watched each week's service on YouTube. My husband would go into the building and preach to an empty sanctuary as our children, and I enjoyed worship at home. Weeks turned into months, and we all felt the strain of this new normal. But for me, it brought a sigh of relief. I didn't need to dodge questions about my mental health. Four months later, our first in-person church service started. Never had I been more nervous to walk into a sanctuary. So many months had elapsed between the time the church closed and the time it reopened, I wasn't sure what to expect. And that's when the panic attacks started again.

As I'm writing this, we are going through a difficult time in our history. Not only are we navigating a pandemic, but racial injustice abounds. I know this creates waves of panic in many of us as we don't know how to navigate this difficult time. However, God is not nervous! Although this seems like a big deal now, one day we will look back and see all God did during this trial. I know this seems counterintuitive, but when those waves of fear radiate through our body, it is a sign we have come to the end of ourselves, and we can cling to him instead.

Beyond helping others as a pastor's wife, the church has done so much for me and poured out such love during my anxious season. I can't emphasize enough the importance of being a part of a local church body. I can't ignore the church's needed presence in my life nor the role it has played in my spiritual growth.

Everyone should be blessed with a church community who will love on them. The cards, gifts, and other special things my church poured out on me after hearing of my diagnosis added so much to lift me up when I was in such a difficult position. Everyone should get to know their members and leaders in their churches. If there ever is a need—reach out! They may pour out their kindness and generosity onto you in such a way you will see, in a tangible way, God's generosity in your life.

LAY DOWN YOUR FEARS

There is so much to learn about surrender from Peter's example in Matthew 14: 22–34, the famous passage about

Peter walking on water:

> Immediately Jesus made the disciples get into the boat and go on ahead of him to the other side, while he dismissed the crowd. After he had dismissed them, he went up on a mountainside by himself to pray. Later that night, he was there alone, and the boat was already a considerable distance from land, buffeted by the waves because the wind was against it. Shortly before dawn Jesus went out to them, walking on the lake. When the disciples saw him walking on the lake, they were terrified. "It's a ghost," they said, and cried out in fear. But Jesus immediately said to them: "Take courage! It is I. Don't be afraid." "Lord, if it's you," Peter replied, "tell me to come to you on the water." "Come," he said. Then, Peter got down out of the boat, walked on the water and came toward Jesus. But when he saw the wind, he was afraid and, beginning to sink, cried out, "Lord, save me!" Immediately Jesus reached out his hand and caught him. "You of little faith," he said, "why did you doubt?"

By now the disciples knew Jesus pretty well. They had spent a considerable time with him. Whenever we spend a significant amount of time with anyone—whether it is our coworkers, spouses, or friends, we begin to know them more intimately. The disciples had spent the day with Jesus, including feeding the multitudes, then he sent them ahead in the boat and disappeared. Now, in their time of need, Jesus is coming to them. But he's coming to them in a way they had not seen before.

The Scriptures say they became fearful of Jesus. Was it because he was at such a considerable distance that they could not make out his facial features, his physical build, or his walk? Was it because the pelting rain and torrential wind were making it hard for them to see anything, let alone Jesus? Whatever the situation, the disciples could not recognize Jesus for who he really was.

Luke 24:36–39 also demonstrates the disciples' inability to recognize who Jesus was:

> While they were still talking about this, Jesus himself stood among them and said to them, "Peace be with you." They were startled and frightened, thinking they saw a ghost. He said to them, "Why are you troubled, and why do doubts rise in your minds? Look at my hands and my feet. It is I myself! Touch me and see; a ghost does not have flesh and bones, as you see I have."

It wasn't until they communed with God and watched him eat in their presence that they understood who he was. They recognized him as they clung to their previous experience of dining with Jesus and the intimacy that had built.

Similarly, in the Exodus passage, the Israelites' fear kept them from believing God would fight for them. They clung to the solution they believed would work— accuse God and Moses of taking them into the wilderness to kill them—instead of asking God for his help and believing he would deliver.

When someone is anxious, high levels of cortisol can affect the brain's ability to function properly. It can cause us not to see situations clearly. The longer the anxiety, the worse the cortisol. Over a prolonged period, cortisol wreaks havoc and can cause a myriad of physical health problems including headaches, digestive issues, thyroid issues, high blood pressure, etc. Anxiety can also be caused by physical ailments in the body. When I had initial blood work taken to see what medication would be best to control my anxiety, they found my thyroid levels were elevated. This in turn can make anxiety flare if left untreated.

Often it is when we cannot see our situations for what

they really are that they cause us to doubt and fear. Doubt and fear are not new to us. These negative emotions have been around since the beginning of time:

> "The woman said to the serpent, "We may eat fruit from the trees in the garden, but God did say, 'You must not eat fruit from the tree that is in the middle of the garden, and you must not touch it, or you will die.'" "You will not certainly die," the serpent said to the woman. "For God knows that when you eat from it your eyes will be opened, and you will be like God, knowing good and evil" (Genesis 3:2–5).

It wasn't that Eve didn't know about the tree: Adam and Eve lived in the garden; they knew about the tree! Her lack of knowledge of what God said was what caused her to fall into sin. Satan twisted her mind into believing God was keeping something from her, that there was pleasure outside of what God had given them, which eventually caused a chain reaction of sin that has affected humanity ever since.

In the Matthew passage, it's not that the disciples didn't know Jesus. The same man whom they spent time with invited them all into a new miracle they had not encountered before. But only Peter decided to join him. The rest knew a God that did the miraculous—they just didn't know he was inviting them into that miracle. Instead of being happy someone was approaching them—and perhaps coming to help them—the disciples turned what they didn't know into an opportunity for fear and doubt. Peter still doubted while he walked on the water; the other disciples were too fearful to even try.

Fear is one of the biggest obstacles to living a surrendered life. Everyone experiences fear from time to time. Fear is a normal reaction to difficult situations or circumstances that might pose a physical, mental, or emotional danger. Our brains take what they perceive as a threat and send signals to our bodies. The disciples perceived Jesus's approach as a threat simply because they couldn't equate what they *saw* with what they *knew*.

PICK UP PERSPECTIVE

Perspective is all about what we perceive. It is one thing to see something, it is quite another to interpret what we see through the lens of reality or past experiences. Jesus is the antidote to a flawed perspective. For example, let's say you hear rumors of people talking badly about you to your friends. This may cause you to become fearful, obsessing over other people's opinions of you. Is what they are saying in sync with what God says about you? Is what they are saying in line with God's Word and his promises for you, or even better, his perception of you?

You may be living in a state of fear right now, but you don't have to stay there. I muddled through a tough season of ongoing panic attacks. But now, by the grace of God, those attacks have stopped. Jesus speaks to us through his Word, and he speaks to our hearts. And this will provide us with a peace that passes all understanding.

OUR HOPE IS IN JESUS

When Jesus said, "Be of good cheer, it is I," he wasn't being condescending or minimizing the trial the disciples were facing. He himself understood this from a young age. He knew his purpose on earth and knew he would face his own trials. He could have been fearful and taken his eyes off his ultimate purpose and work on earth. Instead, he chose to stay close to the Father and focus on what his Father wanted him to do.

Other people from the Bible almost forgot to live out their purposes too. Moses almost didn't use his voice to change the world when he complained he would not have adequate words. Peter forgot his purpose when he denied Christ but was redeemed when God restored him to fellowship. Judas worshipped money rather than the Savior when he sold Christ for money and missed out on the opportunity for Jesus to redeem his eternal life. Paul believed his purpose was to kill Christians to purify the Jewish religion; however, God redeemed Paul's purpose when Paul pointed people to Christ through his words.

I imagine Jesus hoped the disciples would recognize an opportunity to recognize him simply by his comforting words in that moment when they saw him. He may have hoped they would choose to reach out to him and use it as an opportunity to get closer to him. However, instead of crying out for joy, they believed he was a ghost and became fearful.

Do you use your fear as an opportunity to cling to Jesus and recognize him for who he really is? Or do you turn to fear and doubt? Even when you don't see Jesus at work in your life or don't see him for who he truly is, you don't have to turn to fear. Pause and consider how your situation aligns with what you know for sure, not what you perceive. Satan's work is to twist what we know and make us believe something different from the truth. When we know and believe the truth (and ultimately, the one who is the Truth) the fear that would otherwise hinder us will be our weapon to help us thrive.

LAYING IT DOWN

1. Do you struggle with fear or anxiety? In what ways does it affect your life?

2. How does knowing what God thinks of us help battle our fears?

3. How did COVID-19 affect your mental health? Did you discover ways to manage it?

—5—
SURRENDER YOUR DISAPPOINTMENTS

That season of uncontrolled anxiety in early 2020 wasn't easy, but when I was having so many panic attacks, I had to lay down my desires, my feelings, and give them over completely to God. It took great risk—I could lose everything! This is hard when many people who did this in the Bible were either persecuted or even martyred for their faith. Remember, all the disciples who chose to follow Jesus (except for John) were martyred for their faith. It's far from comfortable to lay down our lives knowing we no longer have control over our circumstances.

Lay Down Control

When you are used to feeling in control of your life, it is easier to cling to that control than let someone else—even God—dictate how your life pans out. For example, when you are in an argument, it is easier to wield your words like weapons than it is to allow God to help you tame your tongue. Erica Wiggenhorn, author of *Letting God Be Enough* says, "handing over our fears to God means learning to accept what we cannot comprehend. It means we can stop striving to make sense out of it and surrender in trust that

God knows what He's doing."[1]

No one said the life of a Christian would be easy. Jesus himself said in John 16:33, "I have told you these things, so that in me you may have peace. In this world you will have trouble. But take heart! I have overcome the world."

Pick Up Trust

Many times, I've told myself how hard it is to not only know the Word but also to do it. I've rebelled against being obedient when the Word has stated a command I didn't want to do.

It is more difficult to repent and forgive than it is to simply rattle off a bunch of Scriptures. It is easier to hold on to pride than it is to let it go. It is easier to hold onto a grudge than it is to lay it down. Yet, this is what true disciples are asked to do—lay down everything for the sake of the gospel.

Surrender involves trusting that God knows what is best for your life. As we are reminded in our anchor passage of Exodus 14, the Israelites were led to lay down their weapons so they could allow God to work. If we want God to have access to every area of our lives, we have to stop striving to make our lives turn out the way we want them to. When my life seems out of control, my first instinct is to work harder, doing everything in my power to make life go my way. It is only when I learn to surrender myself to God's will am I most productive.

Kristine B. from Texas shared this story about God's calling for her to surrender what she believed was a calling from him:

> Opening a community outreach facility within a church was a leap of faith unlike any we'd taken before. Our small congregation and team of servant-minded friends came

alongside us for five years, working hard to see it happen. As church planters and pastors, my husband and I poured our hearts, not to mention our time and energy, into this ministry we knew God had called us to. But we were just plain exhausted.

The ministry hit a bumpy patch (or more like a boulder) leaving us short on resources. On top of that, my best friend and longtime children's ministry partner passed away unexpectedly. I didn't have the bandwidth to keep going, but I also didn't want to let the people down. To be honest, *I didn't want to let God down.*

I wanted to work hard for God. Do everything with excellence. But with all those good intentions, I was forgetting to entrust the outcome to a mighty God who works in ways beyond what I can imagine. I had to be willing to let it go, so I surrendered this ministry where I'd given all I could.

Literally the very day the closed sign went up, another local pastor came and knocked on the door. Their church needed a meeting place with more space. Our facility would prove to be a perfect fit for their building needs and heart for outreach. God moved them into a position to keep the community center going while providing them the space they needed for growth. Laying it down also created the space I would need for the next step in my journey. I watched God's faithfulness unfold when I chose to surrender.[2]

I completely relate to this story. So many times, I don't want to disappoint others, but really, the main person I am afraid of disappointing is God. Although it is impossible to disappoint an all knowing, all loving God, I still believe that if I don't perform to his standards, he will withhold or withdraw love from me. This makes me want to work harder and put my trust in my own effort rather than yielding my life to God, allowing him to control the results. This is where the art of surrender comes in. The more I give over my wants and desires to God, the easier it becomes for me to let go of the outcome and trust in God and ultimately engage in the intimate relationship God wants from me.

When disappointments occur, we can learn from our trials. Yield your life to him and resist the urge to just work hard. You'll avoid another disappointment: the disappointment of living a life outside of God's will.

LAYING IT DOWN

1. Even our biggest disappointments in life can humble us and change us for the better. Think of a time or incident that a disappointment has done that for you.

2. In what areas do you need to stop striving in your own effort? How does it make you feel to relinquish control?

3. How do you think God can use your most recent disappointment for his glory?

CHAPTER SIX—SURRENDER YOUR DOUBTS

I saw a Facebook meme the other day that was too good not to share. The picture on the left showed a picture of a cougar with a baby cub in her mouth. From the angle the picture is displayed, it is obvious to any viewer the cougar is eating the cub's head. Yet, the picture on the right, taken from a different angle, tells a whole other story. The same scene, with the picture taken from behind, clearly depicts the cub's head downward and not in the cougar's mouth at all. In fact, it depicts the cougar carrying the cub by the scruff of its neck. The text explaining the picture is poignant: "Your perception of reality depends on what you see and what you are shown. Do some research on your own." This Facebook meme communicates a sobering truth: like I mentioned in chapter four, what we *perceive*, may not always be what *is*.

Lay Down Your Doubts

In the months following my anxiety diagnosis, I was convinced my life as I knew it was over. I doubted I'd ever write again. I was sure I'd never serve in my church. I believed my new normal did not include anything from my former life. As you can see, dear reader, my doubts were proven incorrect.

In Exodus 14, the Israelites shared the same type of doubt as they surveyed the swarm of armies that surrounded them. Everything in them must have wanted to retreat, to run and hide. Surely the battle was over for them! But they forgot one thing: The battle might have been over, but they had the One who already won the war.

Similarly, when my anxiety was at its peak, it was easy to think I had lost. But when my fear was at its worst, it freed me to cling to the arms of Jesus in ways I never thought possible.

Perspective is everything, isn't it? When I'm not anchored in the Word of God, my perspective waxes and wanes with what the world tells me. Satan capitalizes on that opportunity and whispers lies. It's my choice whether I believe those lies. But when I see my circumstances from the perspective of Jesus, I can fight my battles with more confidence because I have someone stronger and more powerful than any adversary. For example, when I am in conflict with another brother or sister in Christ, it is easy for me to see them from my perspective of my hurt feelings and personal bias. But when I pray and ask God to let me see them the way he sees them, I see them with love and compassion.

Pick Up Faith

Jesus is asking us to lay down our doubts and pick up faith. Christians often say during trial, "I just need to have more faith." But even the most faithful will have moments when they take their eyes off Jesus and focus on their circumstances. Although surrender takes faith and believing God will move in the midst of our circumstances, surrender is also about knowing God so intimately we stay focused on him and his promises even if he doesn't move the way we want him to. Just like the Israelites needed to be still and let God work, sometimes the best thing we can do is stretch out our hands, at the end of ourselves, and cry to God for help.

If you are going through a difficult life circumstance, take heart. You might believe your world is falling apart, but God is still in control. When we surrender our lives and will to him, the miraculous can happen. Trust and believe your God. He will fight for you in the moment; you may only need to be still.

LAYING IT DOWN

1. In what area of life have you looked at the physical circumstances rather than concentrating on Jesus? Where has your doubt caused you to take your eyes off Jesus?

2. In what life circumstance is God asking you to lay down your doubts and pick up faith?

3. Has God allowed you to see your situation from his perspective, or do you see it from your perspective? What can you do to see things from his perspective?

CHAPTER SEVEN—SURRENDER YOUR TO-DO LISTS

I love lists.

Lists help me keep order.

Lists help me to organize the most important things in life.

In the first part of this book, we have focused on Moses's command in Exodus 14 to lay weapons down and be still so God could work. But to surrender doesn't only mean to do nothing. As we shall see in the next section, surrender means to lay down your current definition of the Christian life and redefine it so the work you do can give you peace and purpose and give your life as well as others' lives new meaning.

When we look at the long list of items on our perpetual to-do lists, it can cause us to adopt a can-do attitude and a commitment to just manage even more. But trying to get it all done leaves little room for the things that matter most—time with friends and family and realizing our dreams.

LAY DOWN PSEUDO-PRODUCTIVITY

Many of us desire to be extra busy for the purpose of appearing important. Pseudo-productivity is defined as "Productive/non-urgent tasks at inappropriate times."[1] We can fall into pseudo-productivity where we only appear to be doing great things for God and the world. Although we may appear productive, pseudo-productivity doesn't lead to advancing the kingdom. Since God has called us to spend our lives advancing his kingdom and helping others find Jesus too, it would sure help if we knew whether our work mattered to God or was only done in self-effort.

Lay Down Pseudo-Productivity in the Church

So much of the work going on in our churches could go away and the church would be no worse for it. We can run programs, attend weekly Bible study and church on Sunday yet miss the point of the gospel message. We can become so busy doing things for God, we forget to spend time with God, and it is more important than ever to not only introduce the world to Christ but to demonstrate his example.

In most of the churches my husband and I serve, our leadership team would discuss the importance of the current programs at the church. Many members wanted to add more programs to our church: potlucks, Bible studies, and just about anything else that would fill up our already overpacked schedules. While there is nothing inherently wrong with having these programs, too much would keep us busy on the outside, but on the inside, we would be spiritually starved and deprived of the very thing we need the most—intimate, deep connections with the body of Christ.

One of the ways we have found that meets the needs of the church without us becoming overwhelmed is to put a lot of our focus on small groups. This model is one of the best ways to achieve connection between brothers and sisters in Christ. This is where mutual trust, understanding, and connection can happen. This is also where spiritual gifts are best utilized. This is the way we are to edify the body of Christ.

Pick Up Purpose

Work is a good thing! Work not only gives us money in our pockets, but it also gives us purpose the way it did Adam and Eve in the garden. After creating Adam, the first thing God did was put him to work! "The Lord God took the man and put him in the Garden of Eden to work it and take care of it" (Genesis 2:15). Work not only passes the time but it is a way in which we use our time wisely for God. Work was a part of paradise. Work is not to be hated or looked upon with disdain; rather, it is meant to give us purpose and meaning behind our days.

Genesis 2:19–20 says, "Now the Lord God had formed out of the ground all the wild animals and all the birds in the sky. He brought them to the man to see what he would name them; and whatever the man called each living creature, that was its name. So, the man gave names to all the livestock, the birds in the sky and all the wild animals." How exciting it must have been for Adam to receive the role of naming the animals and caring for God's creatures. What an honor! I wonder if Adam felt privileged to be bestowed such an honor, or, if because he was so close to God, it would have been just a part of their life together in the garden. Either way, God designed work so we can be good stewards of what God has given us.

While we are not to define ourselves by it, God wants work to give us purpose and meaning in life. I firmly believe we will work in heaven. Revelation 22:3 says, "No longer will there be any curse. The throne of God and of the Lamb will be in the city, and his servants will serve him." The work will not be by the sweat of our brows like the work we have now due to the curse in Genesis 3. Our work will be a joy for us, capitalizing on our heart's desires and our gifts and talents. But until then, we are to work in whatever

God has called us as if we are working for him in heaven. Colossians 3:23 says, "Whatever you do, work at it with all your heart, as working for the Lord, not for men."

Assess your Work Life

Take a moment and assess the work you do throughout the week as I do regularly. How much of your day centers around work to make money? How much do you use work to maintain—or acquire—possessions? On average, how many hours do you spend on work where you get things done, and how much do you waste scrolling social media and other forms of entertainment? Have you asked God how to make the most of your day to be productive? Ask God to show you how to work smarter rather than harder, taking advantage of the times you have the most energy, so you can give God the best of yourself and accomplish his mission with excellence. Tackle the hardest job when you have the most energy, not at the end of the day, or else you will not be able to dedicate the best of yourself to accomplish the task with excellence. When I shift my perspective to working for God, it transforms work into a precious gift I can give him—even my to-do list.

Laying It Down

1. What is your current view of work? Do you see your work as a way to worship and live as an example of Christ?

2. Look back on your past occupations. Do you believe you saw them as opportunities to make a difference for Christ?

3. What is your current view of work after reading this chapter? How did this chapter change your view?

CHAPTER EIGHT—SURRENDER YOUR WILL

"I don't think I can go without coffee," my husband said as he flipped through the book *The Daniel Fast* by Rick Warren. This past year, we had both been looking for a new way to drop a few pounds and live a healthier lifestyle. But as we skimmed the book's content, we realized we would have to make some serious sacrifices to ensure we followed the plan fully. No coffee, no processed foods. These had been staples of our diet for far too long. We knew it was time for a change. After all, our bodies are supposed to be temples of the Holy Spirit, right? But to change our bodies, we would have to change our minds and hearts, and that would mean not relying on ourselves but on God's strength. It would mean we would have to make tough choices.

LAY DOWN YOUR WILLPOWER

For years, I tried fad diets or exercised by using sheer willpower. We think if we simply want something enough, we can achieve it on our own. The will is hard to battle on our own. Jeremiah 13:23 says, "Can an Ethiopian change his skin or a leopard its spots? Neither can you do good who are accustomed to doing evil." How can we battle our will when it is easily bent toward doing things we know are wrong?

Renewing our minds with the Word of God and enlisting the help of an accountability partner will help when our desires get the best of us.

Doing life on our own is one of Satan's main tricks. He can easily deceive us when we don't have other people who carry spiritual gifts like discernment and wisdom to help us make it through life's toughest decisions. Life is better when we do it together.

In Exodus 14:13, Moses reminds the Israelites that God is still in control: "Moses answered the people, 'Do not be afraid. Stand firm and you will see the deliverance the LORD will bring you today.'" If Moses hadn't been there, and it was merely the Israelites in the midst of battle, would they have been able to stand firm and curb their fear? Accountability partners speak into our lives and give us the truth of God, especially when we are afraid. Accountability partners help us achieve community by being trusted advocates who can handle our weaknesses with grace and help us up when we fall. Over the years, I've found safe people as my accountability partners so I can confess sin and process events and circumstances that become too overwhelming. I'm grateful for them. They see my situation with fresh eyes, and they speak wisdom from their years of experience as a Christian. Every aspect of my life benefits from an accountability partner.

The battle of the human will is universal. Even Jesus had a will, and he had to battle it as well. Despite knowing his identity was secure in the love of his Father, Jesus's human will still tried to pull him away from his Father's will.

We see this in the moments before the crucifixion:

> Then Jesus went with his disciples to a place called Gethsemane, and he said to them, "Sit here while I go over there and pray." He took Peter and the two sons of Zebedee along with him, and he began to be sorrowful and troubled.

I SURRENDER ALL (SORT OF) | 57

> Then he said to them, "My soul is overwhelmed with sorrow to the point of death. Stay here and keep watch with me." Going a little farther, he fell with his face to the ground and prayed, "My Father, if it is possible, may this cup be taken from me. Yet not as I will, but as you will." Then he returned to his disciples and found them sleeping. "Couldn't you men keep watch with me for one hour?" he asked Peter. "Watch and pray so that you will not fall into temptation. The spirit is willing, but the flesh is weak." Matthew 26:36–41

I know what it's like to battle the will. Whether it's the scale, my bank account, or my relationships, my flesh tends to rule my will, which is weak. I want to do the right thing, but my will becomes tempted to take the easy way out, indulge in a temporary pleasure, or think of myself instead of others—unless I remember to focus on Jesus.

Even though Jesus knew the mission behind his coming to earth, he still lived among us as one of us. He knew every temptation we have faced. That's what makes his death and resurrection so meaningful in our lives. He wasn't just a foreign god who didn't understand suffering; he *embodied* suffering, as a human among humans, so we could be set free from the bondage suffering gives us. He understands our situations fully because he has lived through them just like we have. He had no magic up his sleeve; he instead chose to live through each trial, so he could ultimately triumph, giving his Father the glory he came to this earth to give him.

PICK UP EMPTINESS

How did Jesus succeed through every trial he suffered? Philippians 2:5–8:

> In your relationships with one another, have the same mindset as Christ Jesus: who, being in very nature God, did not consider equality with God something to be used to his

own advantage; rather, he made himself nothing by taking the very nature of a servant, being made in human likeness. And being found in appearance as a man, he humbled himself by becoming obedient to death—even death on a cross!

He didn't have to prove anything to anyone—he just had to trust in God to carry him through. He prayed and spent time alone. This was his lifeline—spending time with the Father. He had no obligation to spend time with his Father—he chose to. Although Scripture doesn't tell us what God said or what Jesus heard during those intimate prayer times, we do know Jesus took on the nature of a servant, and that when he prioritized his time with the Father and listened to him, everything else became more bearable.

To become the greatest, Jesus had to become the least. We are called to become like the least if we are to become like him. Jesus emptied himself of all power so that he could become like us on earth. The only way to surrender to God is to empty ourselves of our pride and desire for approval and identity in anything other than Christ.

JESUS WAS TEMPTED

Then Jesus was led by the Spirit into the wilderness to be tempted by the devil. After fasting forty days and forty nights, he was hungry. The tempter came to him and said, "If you are the Son of God, tell these stones to become bread." Jesus answered, "It is written: 'Man shall not live on bread alone, but on every word that comes from the mouth of God.'" Then the devil took him to the Holy City and had him stand on the highest point of the temple. "If you are the Son of God," he said, "throw yourself down. For it is written: 'He will command his angels concerning you, and they will lift you up in their hands, so that you will not strike your foot against a stone.'"

> Jesus answered him, "It is also written: 'Do not put the Lord your God to the test.'" Again, the devil took him to a very high mountain and showed him all the kingdoms of the world and their splendor. "All this I will give you," he said, "if you will bow down and worship me. Jesus said to him, "Away from me, Satan! For it is written: 'Worship the Lord your God and serve him only.'" Then the devil left him, and angels came and attended him. Matthew 4:1–11

Some people believe that to be a Christian means you can't be tempted. But even Jesus was tempted. I can't imagine Jesus, during many days of fasting, didn't desire to eat the bread Satan offered. But Jesus was able to withstand Satan's snares by using a couple of tools:

The Word—Jesus knew the Scriptures; he was an expert in the law. Scripture says he went to the temple to learn as young as twelve years of age. He already knew he needed that bread to feed his soul at a tender age. He also knew he should be learning from teachers and other experts so he would be equipped to carry out God's purpose later in life. In the same way, the Scriptures are what we need to get us through the most difficult parts of life. When all hope seems lost, and our lives are turned upside down, we can rely on the Word of God that has been etched into our hearts to combat Satan's schemes.

The world can so easily turn our hearts to worship the wrong things rather than God. Jesus not only knew the Word but also the principles in it. Scripture should be on the tip of our tongues as well. it is impossible to defeat Satan if we don't have the precepts of the Bible in our hearts and minds.

I want to encourage you to make even a small effort to memorize and understand the Scriptures. It is within every Christian's grasp to follow Jesus's example and to spend intentional time with the Father through prayer and the Word. This reminds us our identity is in Jesus.

Satan is crafty, but his temptations often hit upon three main areas: popularity, pride, and others' approval (1 John 2:16). If our identities aren't secure in who God has made us, we will always fall for Satan's schemes. Jesus knew who he was and *whose* he was. It was enough for him to have his Father declare, "My beloved son, whom I love, with him I am well pleased" (Matthew 3:17), and no matter what Satan threw at him, Jesus resisted. Adam and Eve were secure in God's love too. When Satan cast doubt on God's instructions, however, they found their identity in prideful knowledge. As a result, they believed they were missing out on life instead of trusting that God gave them all they needed to be happy.

To live a life of surrender and survive the battle of the will, we must pick up emptiness. It takes humbling ourselves and emptying ourselves of any arrogance or the false idea we can handle life on our own. When we anchor ourselves by knowing the Word of God, we will be able to better handle the temptations that come our way.

LAYING IT DOWN

1. In what areas of your life do you battle your will? How do you handle the temptations that come your way?

2. Describe a time when you tried to overcome a challenge using sheer willpower? What happened?

3. Reconsider the same scenario from the previous question. How would that situation have been different if you had emptied yourself of your willpower and relied on God to get you through?

CHAPTER NINE—SURRENDER YOUR PRIDE

Arrogance can creep into our lives undetected. It is the stumbling block that makes us focus on the wrong areas of life. Pride wants us to look good to others—so much so, we lose sight of the important things in life.

In my book, *Righteous and Lost*, I talk about the eldest brother's role in the parable of the lost son. Although the prodigal is the focus of the parable, there is so much about the eldest brother we can learn, even though there is so little explicitly stated. For example, why did the eldest brother stay to work the father's field when he had already been given his part of the inheritance? It is clear in the beginning the father gave both what he had been saving for them, yet only one spent it. Then, after the prodigal brother returns, it's the eldest brother who is seen "slaving in the field." For what? Wasn't he already rich? He didn't have to stay. The father let them both off the hook to be responsible for the father's possessions, yet the eldest brother stays. He initially sounds noble, but if he was going to stay, why did he complain? The eldest son's pride kept him as lost as the prodigal son. His pride kept him in the field slaving away, pretending he cared about his father's field, but his complaints showed he didn't care at all. The eldest was just as lost as the prodigal, he just hid it better. The prodigal's impulsiveness and lack of self-control was his downfall. The eldest brother's pride was his.[1]

In the moments of my panic attacks, I could barely keep my sanity, let alone hold onto any pride. I could no longer think of myself as better than anyone. I couldn't do life on my own but only rely on others to help me function. By showing my uncontrolled self to others, Jesus stripped me of any remnant of conceit and vanity.

This is what Jesus intends for us—to rid ourselves of any conceit or thought only of ourselves. Jesus said, "Therefore if you have any encouragement from being united with Christ, if any comfort from his love, if any common sharing in the Spirit, if any tenderness and compassion, then make my joy complete by being like-minded, having the same love, being one in spirit and of one mind. Do nothing out of selfish ambition or vain conceit. Rather, in humility value others above yourselves, not looking to your own interests but each of you to the interests of the others" (Philippians 2:1–3). Furthermore, 1 Peter 5:5 says, "Likewise, you who are younger, be subject to the elders. Clothe yourselves, all of you, with humility toward one another, for 'God opposes the proud but gives grace to the humble.'"

On the surface, the eldest brother had every reason not to be gracious to the youngest son. Let's consider for a second how the prodigal's request might have looked to everyone in the community. To ask for your inheritance early was to figuratively spit in the father's face. It was saying, "Dad. You're not enough. I want your money." How it must have grieved the father to give the money to his sons, knowing they wanted him only for what he could give, not for who he was. Yet, he gave it anyway.

As the firstborn son, he was already, by rights, entitled to the father's estate. Because the son was so focused on what he didn't get (the party, but more importantly, the celebration and honor of the prodigal's life), he loses focus on all he already received.

The father was, in essence, giving them the choice to choose him or choose the money. The prodigal chose the money. The eldest chose both the money and the work. Neither chose the father's love. The difference is that the prodigal came to his senses and repented. It's not until his about face that the father runs off to greet him. The prodigal wasn't moving *away* from the father's love but *toward* it.

It's the same with us. If we understood all that we have inherited by being sons and daughters of the King, would we be obsessed with jealousy and envy of what everyone else has? The Israelites wanted to battle the army on their own. But when they see Pharaoh and his armies, they realize they are outnumbered.

"They said to Moses, "Was it because there were no graves in Egypt that you brought us to the desert to die? What have you done to us by bringing us out of Egypt? Didn't we say to you in Egypt, 'Leave us alone; let us serve the Egyptians'? It would have been better for us to serve the Egyptians than to die in the desert!" (Exodus 14:11–12). They are afraid of death, but instead of facing their fear and crying out to God, they turn on Moses through their pride and basically say, "Told you so! This is too much! Why didn't you just leave us alone like we told you to?" They try to shift blame until Moses tells them to surrender their fear and pride and simply "stand firm" (v.13). Stand firm in the truth of who God is. Stand firm in his sovereignty. Stand firm in his faithfulness.

Is God asking you to surrender an area of your life where pride has crept in and simply stand firm in the truth of the promises of God?

Lay Down Your Reputation

"Michelle, will you come to the guidance counselor's office." The loudspeaker barked these words one Tuesday morning. As a sophomore in high school, I had never been called to the counselor's office before, so I had never been called over the loudspeaker. I was shocked and scared at why she might want to see me. I sat in the chair and listened to the counselor. "Well, according to your grades, you qualify to be a part of our honors English class." I was good at English (a shocker for a future writer) so I was excited at the opportunity. "But here's the thing. If you go into our honors English class, you must transfer into our honors history class as well."

I wasn't too bad at history. I had to work hard to remember dates and events, but I figured it was a great opportunity. I figured I'd just work harder, and I'd succeed. I did well in the English class with a bit of hard work. But the history class was brutal. No matter how hard I tried, I couldn't get a good grade. I'd study for weeks, memorizing notes and highlighting most words on every page of the textbook. Before the first test, the teacher explained the rules. "I only give the test verbally. I read the questions out loud, and you write your answers in the blanks. This way, you can't cheat by reading it off another's paper. No whiteout. No erasers. If you make a mistake, it is marked wrong. I only repeat the questions once, then you will have time at the end if you need a question repeated. And don't be absent. My makeup tests are composed of all essays and the test is ten times harder than the regular test."

As someone who struggles with anxiety, this kept me up the night before each test in a state of panic. The day of the test came, and I got a 68. I was devastated. Then, the teacher began making inappropriate comments to the girls. The comments began to make most of us girls uncomfortable. This became enough for me to struggle with anxiety all the time. I often came home with headaches, an upset stomach, etc. I was afraid to tell anyone about what I was experiencing in the classroom. Between the failing grades and the comments, the class was becoming unbearable.

My mother noticed I wasn't eating, and as I often complained of headaches, she knew something was wrong. For many months I said everything was fine, until I couldn't take it anymore, and I told her everything. She called the school and set up an appointment to speak to the history teacher along with the assistant principal.

The day came for the meeting. I walked down the long hallway to the administrative offices at the end of the school day at two o'clock. My mother had already arrived and was seated in the chair outside the office. As we sat in silence, we could hear the teacher already in with the assistant principal. They laughed uproariously. Were they laughing at us?

We were called in and began discussing the situation. The teacher listened at first. Then my mom said something that set him off: "I think my daughter is intimidated by you."

At that, he flung his head back and laughed out loud. Then he banged on the side of the principal's metal desk, pointed his finger, and said, "If she can't hack it in my class, that's her problem, not mine." He went on to compare me to other more intelligent kids in the class, making it seem the reason I wasn't doing well was simply because I wasn't smart enough to be a part of the honors class. My mother and I sat in silence, stunned at what the teacher had just done.

"Well, normally we don't do this," the assistant principal explained. "If you decided to leave the history class, you would have to leave the English class too. But because you are doing well in English, we will let you transfer to the regular history class if you decide. Let us know what you choose to do."

We went to the car and sat in silence. "I can't believe you were telling the truth," my mom said after a long pause. "You were telling the truth the whole time. In fact, it was worse than what you said it was." After a moment of silence, she continued, "Your father and I will support whatever you do."

At first, I wanted to stay. I had earned the grades to be in the honors history class, and I wasn't going to let that teacher take it away from me. I decided to stay in the class and try again.

About two days before the next test, I came down with bronchitis and missed the test. My anxiety went through the roof! The only way I could guarantee a decent grade was to study. I studied hard, memorized notes, and highlighted my textbook. I memorized the notes so well I could turn the page with my eyes closed because I knew my notes continued on the next page! But when the test came, it was a whole different story. There were names and dates on it that I had never seen before. I wasn't shocked to receive a thirty-two on my test. At this point, I had one choice—to leave in disgrace and humiliation.

I transferred to the regular history class. As I walked to class, the kids from the honors class snickered in the hall. Of course, everyone knew I had transferred out of class. Soon the weeks passed, and I had the last test of my history class. I went to my teacher and asked how I had done. He opened the grade book and closed it. "You got a 100." He was someone who liked to make jokes in class, so I assumed he was kidding. "What? I got a 100?" I stared at him in disbelief.

He opened the book and pointed to my name and grade. "See, look." I couldn't believe it. At that moment, he noticed my other history teacher walking into the teacher's lounge.

"Looks like your former teacher went into the lounge," he said. He then nodded to the hall pass and said, "I think the bathroom next to the lounge is free."

I knew what he was saying. I called the history teacher out of the lounge into the hallway. "Just so you know, I got a 100 on my final."

"Well, that's great," my teacher said flippantly and walked into the lounge. Even though he blew me off, it was satisfying to have proven him wrong about me.

PICK UP HUMILITY

Humility is defined as "a modest or low view of one's own importance."[1] The prodigal had to swallow his pride and ask for help with a posture of repentance. The Lord fought for me in my history class, but to do so, I had to surrender my pride. Pride is the antithesis to humility. As long as our pride rules us, we can never humble ourselves to ask for help. We allow ourselves to isolate rather than rely on the community to keep us accountable.

We all need others to help us along in our journey. Humility allows God and others to fight for us and allows me to put others first before myself.

God used that history class experience not only to humble me but also to enlist the help of my mother. I was able to open up to her and express what was going on, which had been difficult for me. When I enlisted the help of my family, it opened the opportunity to express myself to my teacher and stand up for the truth—even if he denied it in the end. This took a posture of humility. Like my history class, the Lord will often take us out of our comfort zones to accomplish his work.

Although that was a pivotal moment in my life where I experienced redemption in the midst of surrender, I had to relearn that lesson when my panic attacks worsened.

It wasn't until I surrendered my reputation (or how I

appeared to others) that I was able to embrace fully the Father's love for me. Never in my life had I experienced God's grace more than in those moments. When anxiety flares, it makes it difficult to concentrate, and behavior can become erratic. I had to rely on the help of my family, church, and others to get me through that difficult time. In a sense, I had hit a rock bottom, just like the prodigal. The prodigal found himself eating the pods that pigs eat. He had nothing left but garbage to eat. When I was able to surrender my reputation in others' eyes, I was able to embrace the Father's love for me.

It is when we step out in obedience, surrender our reputation, and agree to go to places we have never gone before that God blesses us the most. We are truly free when we let God decide who we are and choose to believe God has taken away our sin and still loves us despite our mistakes. When we live a life of surrender, we no longer must hide under a mask of pride. We can be free. This means I no longer have to appear as if I do everything right or am perfect. The pressure is off!

Laying It Down

1. What examples can you think of in the Bible that discuss letting go of pride?

2. Has there been a time when you have had to surrender your reputation? What emotions did you feel when you did this?

3. The opposite of pride is humility. What area of your life does God want you to admit you need help with and ask others for help?

CHAPTER TEN—SURRENDER YOUR DEVOTIONS

Read my Bible. Check.
Prayed for various prayer requests. Check.
Spent five minutes in silence. Check.

Putting my Bible in its slot near my favorite chair in the living room after my devotion time, I patted myself on the back—figuratively of course. By all outside appearances, I was the good Christian girl. I was doing the right thing, putting God first in the morning before proceeding with my day. But the position of my Bible at that moment was symbolic of my internal life: God had his place, but once I put him in his spot in my mind, he rarely entered it again until the next day when it was time to check off my to-do list.

Don't get me wrong. There is nothing wrong with having a daily devotional time. In fact, no Christian life can flourish without it. I wasn't doing anything wrong, but my priorities were off-balance. Although I was doing my devotions, I wasn't devoting my life to God.

See the difference?

Jesus didn't just set aside time in the morning before he went to work driving out demons and healing the sick. He surrendered his life to the will of the Father. Nothing in his life was apart from the Father's will. He let nothing stand in the way of what he was called by his Father to do while on earth—heal the sick, drive out demons and preach the gospel.

How do we live a life devoted to the Father's will when we have so many other demands vying for our time and attention?

LAY DOWN OBLIGATIONS

We will always have something demanding our time and attention. But work and the busyness of life don't have to monopolize our time. Jesus said in Mark 12:17, "give to Caesar what is Caesar's, and to God what is God's." Although that is referring mostly to taxes, it has a general concept we can follow as well. We will always be obligated to the world we live in, whether it is to the government, our boss, or our children. However, God deserves the first fruits of our lives. Just as in Malachi 3:8–10 we are instructed to give the fruits of what God has provided, in the same way, we should also give him the first part of our time and attention:

> "Will a mere mortal rob God? Yet you rob me. But you ask, 'How are we robbing you?' In tithes and offerings. You are under a curse—your whole nation—because you are robbing me. Bring the whole tithe into the storehouse, that there may be food in my house. Test me in this," says the Lord Almighty, "and see if I will not throw open the floodgates of heaven and pour out so much blessing that there will not be room enough to store it."

We want to live lives devoted to God as the disciples did, but our lifestyle looks little like the disciples of biblical times. The disciples of the Bible were able to spend their lives preaching the gospel, driving out demons, and healing the sick. Since times have changed, what would giving God our first fruits of time, talents, and abilities look like in today's demanding world? Perhaps it would mean emptying out our savings account to help a family in need. Maybe it means sacrificing Sundays to visit the sick in the hospital. Whatever God might be calling you to do, it may look like a stark contrast to the comfortable Christianity we are used to.

We live in a country where we are still free to read and study the Bible and preach it to the masses, using various forms of verbal and written communication. How can we use modern technology to preach the gospel to the unsaved? How can we work with other like-minded Christians, so we look more similar to the disciples of Jesus's day?

Pick Up Abiding in Christ

A life of devotion and surrender is only possible when we stay focused on Christ's presence in our lives, realizing we can't survive without him. John 15:1–7 speaks to the necessity of staying close to God, for without him we can do nothing:

> I am the true vine, and my Father is the gardener. He cuts off every branch in me that bears no fruit, while every branch that does bear fruit, he prunes so that it will be even more fruitful. You are already clean because of the word I have spoken to you. Remain in me, as I also remain in you. No branch can bear fruit by itself; it must remain in the vine. Neither can you bear fruit unless you remain in me. I am the vine; you are the branches. If you remain in me and I in you, you will bear much fruit; apart from me you can do nothing. If you do not remain in me, you are like a branch that is thrown away and withers; such branches are picked up, thrown into the fire and burned. John 15:1–6

According to this passage, Christ's first job after lifting us up is to prune us. Anything that is not helping us bear fruit in his name is considered a hindrance to our growth and must be cut off. But pruning is hard! God often allows the hard in our lives so he can make us more like him. Even though pruning is painful and tough, the good parts that remain are the ones God uses to produce Christlike character within us.

In my twenty-one years of being a pastor's wife, my husband and I have encountered our share of conflict and strife within our churches. During the first year of any new church, my husband establishes vision and mission for the church, then trims back the programs and other areas of church life that are not focused on the mission or vision. But this does not come without strife and conflict with those who are comfortable participating in those programs. Sometimes it even results the loss of church members because they disagree with this vision. It is difficult for me to lose many wonderful people from our churches. Although conflicts sometimes remain unresolved and reconciliation is not possible, I learned that my way doesn't always have to be the only way. During these times, I have learned to not sweat the small stuff and to choose my battles carefully. I must make sure if we are going to cut a church ministry, it's worth losing people.

But loss and trial are often what Christ uses to prune us and make us more like him. By pruning away my pride and need to be right, Christ's pruning has helped me become more merciful and gracious. It also has taught me humility as it's hard not to assert my belief that I am right even when others disagree. Trials are never easy, but when I come through them, I notice I am different from when I started. We begin to see more fruit of the Spirit emerge (Galatians 5:22–23) as more perseverance and character develop as a result.

Christ's second job is to feed us. A branch has to stay attached to its vine to receive the water and nutrients it needs to grow. When it gets detached from its source of nutrients, it doesn't take long before it dies. It's the same with us. When we reduce our devotional time to whatever is left over from our overpacked schedule, we detach ourselves from the source of our nutrients which are essential to our growth.

Devotions do not need to be limited to a small block of time. God wants all of us, not just a sliver of time from our day. What would it look like if we were able to commune with God twenty-four hours a day, seven days a week?

Often by the time we get home from work, we are exhausted, leaving little time to spend time in prayer. Our human bodies and minds are limited, needing rest and recuperation after a long day. Can we adjust our day to make more room for God while recognizing our limitations? For example, can we get more sleep at night to finish our days earlier, so we can start earlier? If mornings don't work, can we capitalize on our waking hours to make more room to focus on the Lord? Can we change our music playlist to be more God honoring? Can we watch one less TV program to make more room for relationships, so we can make disciples?

Analyze a typical day. What can you do with the spare minutes while you are stuck in traffic? Can you change your morning routine to make more room for God? Can you listen to a podcast or read a book while exercising? Can you eat healthier to mold your body into the temple it is supposed to be? How can you devote your life to God by being a better witness to the person at work that gives you the most trouble?

The possibilities are endless; we just have to open our minds and challenge our previous ways of thinking.

Each of us has the choice to spend time doing what we feel God is most calling us to or living for ourselves and wasting the opportunities God has put in front of us. Sometimes it takes intentionality and perseverance to develop new habits that use our time wisely and make the most of the opportunities with God. Imagine the joy and contentment we could experience if we dedicated more of our time to God. We all have a choice; what we do with our time is up to us. Jesus sought opportunities to change people's lives and the fruit of his life is still felt today.

TRY SPIRITUAL DISCIPLINES

One way to go to the next level in our relationship with God is to develop a new spiritual discipline. Even the most dedicated Christian can experience dry times with God where they feel he is silent and distant. But spiritual disciplines can help get us out of a spiritual rut and into a new encounter. Below I list some spiritual disciplines that may sound foreign but can easily be implemented into a daily routine. I want to encourage you to pray and ask God which one he would like you to try and see if you experience God in a new way:

Solitude (Mark 1:35): Finding space to be in the presence of God alone, free from distractions, with no agenda other than to be alone with him.

Tips:
- Schedule it in your calendar.
- Find a place free from distractions.
- Resist the temptation to "do anything." Simply "be in his presence." The goal is not to achieve a result but rather simply be in his presence.

Silence (Psalm 46:10): Being completely quiet and still before God, without talking or allowing your mind to wander (but if it does wander, grab a notebook and write down thoughts that you are having difficulty ridding yourself of.)

I SURRENDER ALL (SORT OF) | 79

Tips:
- Schedule a time and place.
- Start small. Two to five minutes may seem long if you've never practiced silence before.
- Use a timer. It will help you avoid being distracted wondering how much time is left.
- If your mind wanders, reflect on a phrase like "be still."

Prayer (1 Thessalonians 5:17): Conversing with God. This involves speaking aloud or thinking and listening.

Tips:
- Set aside any expectations of hearing specifically from God.
- Try making a prayer list to present your needs before him.
- Learn from Jesus's prayer (Luke 11:1–13).
- Practice listening, not just talking.
- Take a journal and write down any stray thoughts. Once your mind is clear, think about a verse and repeat it to yourself. Pray and invite God to speak to you. You may hear from him; you may not. It is not a magic formula. You are making room for God in your daily life, not manipulating him to speak within your limitations.

Study (Psalm 1:1–3): Engaging with the written Word of God at a deeper level than simply reading.

Tips:
- Schedule a time and place.
- Study complete sections, paragraphs, stories, and entire books of the Bible.
- Meditate on what you're reading: see the sights, hear the sounds, feel the emotions.
- Use Bible commentaries.
- Take notes.

Worship (Revelation 4:11): Ascribing "worth" to God by expressing his greatness, beauty, and goodness.

Tips:
- Schedule a time and place.
- If you're musical, use an instrument. If not, use any device to listen to music.
- Stretch yourself. Use both new music (Psalm 40:3) and familiar favorites.
- List the attributes of God. Choose songs that emphasize these characteristics.

Celebration (2 Samuel 6:12–16): Celebrating and enjoying ourselves, our lives, and our world as God's gift to us.

Tips:
- Schedule a time and place.
- Practice different ways of celebrating: write down what you are celebrating, share with someone else, take a walk, reflect on God's gifts, dance, etc. Be creative!

Growing Service (Colossians 3:23–24): Engaging in activities that promote the good of others and the mission of God in our world.

Tips:
- Make sure you are serving out of selflessness and not for selfish reasons or human applause.
- Select something that is practical.
- Volunteer in a place within your community where you can simply be a blessing. This will help you be the hands and feet of God right where you live.

Confession (James 5:16): Confessing our deepest weaknesses and failures to someone.

I SURRENDER ALL (SORT OF) | 81

Tips:
- Find someone you can trust.
- Schedule a regular time to connect and confess.
- Give that person permission to ask you hard questions.
- We are called to confess our sins to one another as in 1 John 9. This helps us to be transparent with others as well as with God. When we do so, we promote unity and emphasize empathy.

Journaling (Daniel 7:1): Writing down the things that are on your heart, the things God is revealing to you, etc.

Tips:
- Schedule a time and place.
- Don't put expectations about how much to write.
- Write about the things you're learning and experiencing.
- Try journaling your emotions: What are you feeling? Why do you think you're feeling this way? Ask God to help you reflect. It's difficult to surrender something to God if I don't know what I'm clinging to.

Sabbath (Deuteronomy 5:15): Setting aside a day to focus and reflect on God, realign with God's kingdom, refresh, remember our true identities, and review our lives.

Tips:
- Schedule a day of the week that works for you.
- Decide how you will rest and what will you rest from (cell phone, electronics, work, email, etc.).
- Decide what activities you will engage in to reset your focus on God and allow him to replenish your soul (read a book, jog, take a walk, watch a movie, etc.).

Scripture Memory (Psalm 119:11): Memorizing verses or books of Scripture.

Tips:
- Start small with a verse or two.
- Use index cards and put the reference on one side and the verse on the other.
- Post the verses in places where you normally interact. This will help focus your mind on God's Word throughout the day. Besides prayer, there is no other way to renew our minds and combat the lies Satan tells us than with the truth of God's word.

Fasting (Matthew 6:17–18): Abstaining from food or a particular activity for a set period.

Tips:
- Start small. Try abstaining from a particular kind of food (or perhaps eat just vegetables for a day) or fasting for one meal. Then work up to two meals, etc. Make sure you drink water.
- Try fasting from activities like TV, cell phone, Facebook, etc. Fasting brings us closer to God because, like Jesus, we must rely on God for our daily bread.

When we try new things in our journey like spiritual disciplines, it helps us cling to Jesus and hear from him in new and exciting ways. If we abide in Christ, we dedicate our lives to him, get rid of the obligations, and spend our lives in the freedom to take whatever God is calling us to do.

Laying It Down

1. What was your understanding of abiding in Christ before you read this chapter? How has it changed because of this chapter?

2. How can I keep my constant, abiding, relationship with Christ fresh through my many obligations?

3. What one new spiritual discipline stood out to you? How can you implement it into your everyday life?

CHAPTER ELEVEN—SURRENDER YOUR IDENTITY

Do you remember how Peter's experience walking on water helps us picture our own life of surrender, no matter the cost? When Peter asks Jesus to call him before he steps out of the boat, he says "Lord, *if* it is you ..." Why did Peter not immediately distinguish Jesus's voice? In this moment, Peter has trouble with Jesus's identity, much as he would have trouble during Jesus's trial when he doesn't want to be associated with Jesus. But Jesus never had trouble understanding his identity. From the moment of his baptism, God solidifies his testimony that Jesus is his son, and he is pleased with him.

When we build our identities on the truth that we are sons and daughters of the King and heirs of God, we will be able to carry out the work of our Father just like Jesus did. But when we build our identities on shifting circumstances—like raging waters—we will surely sink.

When Jesus said, "It is I. Do not be afraid," Peter believed him. He believed so strongly that, when Jesus said, "Come," he was willing to lay down everything in his life, leave the relative safety of the boat, and put his weight on the troubled surface of the water. Even if Peter doubted his ability to walk on water in his own strength, he put his faith in Jesus, allowing his identity as a son of God to be enough for him. When we build our lives on the belief Jesus is not enough, like Peter as he turned his eyes to the wind, this is when we get into trouble. Jesus in his compassion rescues us from our fear and doubt. The more we allow Jesus to be enough for us, the less we will sink back into shifting circumstances, and the more opportunities we will have to proclaim the gospel to the masses.

Jesus never wrestled with his identity because his identity was rooted in being God's son. That was all he needed. His knowledge of his Father was enough to avoid the trap of comparison and inferiority. As humans, we all struggle with the temptation of defining ourselves by our possessions, our popularity, or our performance. Anything in which we find our view of ourselves becomes an idol. Whether we worry about what people think, what we own, or how much we do, we easily put our identities in the hands of something fleeting. Even though it's foolish to depend on the fickle things around us rather than on the unchanging love of God, we still find ourselves too often gliding down a slippery slope of disappointment.

Lay Down Others' Approval

We cannot live a surrendered life if we build our identities on things that don't matter. While God may choose to bless us with material possessions and other rewards, this should not, and does not, define who we are. We cannot be searching for identity in anything other than who God is.

Peter wrestled with his identity too. But when Jesus called him out of the boat, Peter's one brief thought of Jesus was enough for him to risk walking on water. "But Jesus immediately said to them: 'Take courage! It is I. Don't be afraid.' 'Lord, if it's you,' Peter replied, 'tell me to come to you on the water'" (Matthew 14:27–28). Jesus knew Peter would care too much about his reputation to acknowledge him in front of the crowds later, yet Jesus chooses to call out to Peter and give him the opportunity to follow in his footsteps and experience a miracle.

A surrendered life always requires being willing to allow our reputations to be tarnished by associating with others for the sake of Christ. This may mean hanging out with people whom Christians may think are beyond God's grace. It is easy in today's world to hang around with people who think, act, and look like us. But Jesus hung out with tax collectors, thieves, and harlots. When we build relationships with such people, we risk being ridiculed by others because they associate us with Jesus. While we may not have the opportunity to eat dinner with prostitutes or thieves, we do need to minister to those whom others think are too far from God, even if we are persecuted because of it.

The Pharisees hated Jesus because he drew the crowd's attention away from the religious leaders—casting them not as honored scholars but yesterday's leftovers. Because of this, the Pharisees allowed jealousy and envy to creep into their hearts. The more we care about how we look to the outside world, the more we give ground for Satan to reign in our lives.

Our reputation is built on a shaky foundation if we build our standing on what other people think of us. By the world's standards, at the time of his death Jesus was one of the most unsuccessful leaders in the world. Yet, no matter whether the crowds came or went, he was rooted in his identity as God's son. It didn't matter even if the twelve disciples were with him or not. All he needed was to know whose son he was.

Pick Up Wholeness

A life of surrender is a life spent pursuing wholeness, without which we end up just a fraction of the person God wants us to be. When we believe Jesus is enough, we live in such a way that we make the most of every moment. We are free to pursue healthy habits that will improve us in every area. We understand our responsibility to care for (and be good stewards of) what God has given us. This includes our physical, mental, emotional, and spiritual health. Jesus did a good job of making sure people's physical needs were met as well as their mental and spiritual health. He multiplied the loaves and fishes and fed the multitudes before sending them away. God designed every part of our being to work synergistically with each other.

Having a healthy mind, body, and spirit is vital to living a whole life. Jesus took time to go to solitary places, to pray and eat well, and take care of himself so he could continue to do the work of his Father. When we neglect to take care of ourselves in one area, other areas of our life will be affected. For example, someone who has unaddressed deep, emotional wounds will eventually have physical health problems, as the emotional issues will affect their physical health. Mental health issues are just as vital to address as physical and emotional concerns.

Physical Health

First Corinthians 6:19–20 says, "Do you not know that your bodies are temples of the Holy Spirit, who is in you, whom you have received from God? You are not your own; you were bought at a price. Therefore, honor God with your bodies." Our bodies are precious vessels, they deserve to be treated with care. It is easy when we are not doing well emotionally, mentally, or spiritually to fill our soul's hunger with junk food and not care for ourselves as well as we should. Additionally, in the life of my church, many social events revolve around food. These events can create a cozy, welcoming atmosphere for members and meet people's needs for community and connection. Having said this, many comfort food dishes are served at these events. These calorie-dense dishes are rich in ingredients that would add weight, not to mention, cholesterol to my diet, and wreak havoc on my body. Making healthier choices can be difficult, but we can lead the way in good eating by bringing foods that are filled with more nutrition than calories.

Mental Health

One of the most important elements in a Christian's mental health is self-talk. Self-talk is the "tape" or self-conscious chatter that plays in our head. What we say to ourselves is important and Scripture tells us we need to renew our minds regularly: "Do not conform any longer to the pattern of this world but be transformed by the renewing of your mind" (Romans 12:2). The Bible is good at revealing God's promises of who we are in Christ. Although you may have read the Bible many times, do you believe what the Bible says about you, or are you allowing the world and your past to shape you?

Self-talk statements can be positive or negative and can shape you as early as childhood. Sometimes statements like, "I'll never amount to anything" or "God can never use me because of what I have been through" creep in. No matter how close to the Lord I feel, there are moments when I slip and accept the world's definition of who I am. But through memorizing God's Word and the support of my church community, I have learned to record over these tapes.

Jesus well understood another aspect of mental health. Even though he had a close relationship with his Father, he still carved time out to spend with him. After he sent the apostles into the boat, he went to a private place to pray. Jesus longed for fellowship with his Father and made the time to engage in it. This was important to him, and he made it a priority even though he was aware a storm was brewing, and the disciples might need him. To be in a good spot mentally, he needed to talk to his Father.

In the same way, we need to talk to our Father too. For good mental health, we need to make time for listening and talking to God. The disciples were sent into a storm, having only their earlier conversations with Jesus to sustain them. To make it through our own day, we need to regularly talk with our Father. This doesn't just mean to pray but to read the Bible as God's love letter to us too. Like Jesus's calming words to his disciples on the sea, his Word can sustain us when we hit life's everyday storms too.

EMOTIONAL HEALTH

Feelings follow thoughts. When our thoughts are set on God, our emotions will follow. However, when we let sin creep in, it affects our thoughts, and our emotions match our thoughts. Our hearts cannot be trusted, as Jeremiah 17:9 says, "The heart is deceitful above all things and beyond cure. Who can understand it?" In secular culture, many movies, songs, and TV shows say, "Follow your heart." This is a slippery slope as our thoughts and feelings are connected. If the heart can be deceived so easily, I need God's help to tether it to him and his Word, so it can be shaped appropriately.

The heart can be fickle as it flits from emotion to emotion based on current circumstances. Yet, when I surrender my heart by anchoring it to the Word of God, it is no longer easily swayed, and I don't fall prey to the devil's schemes.

Pick Up Openness

Jesus wants to experience life with us. We don't need to physically walk on water to have intimate moments with the Savior. We can achieve the same intimacy and act in the same humility through daily interactions with Jesus. Whether it is reading the Word, praying, listening, or practicing spiritual disciplines, we can all have a moment of "walking on water" when we step out in faith, cry out to God, and take his hand, and go where he is leading us.

One Sunday, my husband gave us an assignment at the end of the sermon. He encouraged us to have a moment where we practiced listening to God. He encouraged us not to talk to him but just listen. When I listened, he first wanted me to confess sin, which I did. Then he spoke to me about my time with him—that it gave him joy when I just sat with him. When I opened my eyes and the service ended, I was on cloud nine! This was an intimate moment with the Savior separate from mere Bible reading and prayer. Jesus had blessed me with hearing from him simply because I chose to make space to spend time in his presence.

Can you recall incredible moments when you enjoyed a moment with the Savior where you just spent time together? How did you feel? Did you feel loved? accepted? valued? This is what the Savior wants for all of us. He wants us to seek time with him just for the sake of enjoying each other's fellowship. This is a part of true success in the kingdom. When we take the time to spend time with the Father simply because we want to and not because of what he does for us, we understand true intimate fellowship with him. If we yield our lives to Christ, even in the moments of failure, he promises to pick us up, redirect us and help us begin a new chapter in our lives.

Get out of the boat, take the first steps, and walk toward Jesus. Even if we sink, Jesus still holds our hand and walks with us step-by-step. He promises he will always be with us no matter what happens. No one will be able to stand against you all the days of your life. "As I was with Moses, so I will be with you; I will never leave you nor forsake you."

And that's the best place to be.

LAYING IT DOWN

1. In what areas of your health do you need to move toward wholeness?

2. Where do you tend to root your identity?

3. How can you change these focuses so you can become rooted in God?

4. It's so easy to see ourselves from others' perspectives. Do you see where your identity truly lies after reading this chapter?

CHAPTER TWELVE—SURRENDER YOUR VISION

"It's OK not to know everything."

I read this statement in a book on mindfulness, and the words jumped off the page at me. Mindfulness includes focusing your mind on a certain phrase to keep from dwelling on negative, anxious thoughts. To calm my anxiety, I often want to know the vision behind a plan before I jump into something. Knowing everything eliminates the risk of being blindsided by difficult circumstances and allows me to prepare for every future scenario.

One of the tools I learned during my anxiety is the power of repeating positive affirmations. "It's OK not to know everything," was my favorite. I wrote it down and taped it to my mirror. For many weeks, as soon as I woke up, I looked myself in the eye and said those words out loud. I was reminded that God would reveal what I needed to know in his time, not in mine. Additionally, another statement I focused on is "It's OK not to be OK." It calmed my soul to know that just because I struggled with a mental health issue didn't mean I should demean myself by believing I was "less than."

This is the essence of our relationship with God. Proverbs 29:18 says, "Where there is no prophetic vision the people cast off restraint but blessed is he who keeps the law" (ESV).

Vision is necessary to move forward in life. But which vision do we use? Sometimes, when circumstances cloud our lives, we lose our vision. Other times God doesn't present his vision to us right away, and it can be hard to even know how to surrender to him. This forces us to trust him and surrender to his will rather than walking in our will and creating our own vision for our lives. When facing the Red Sea and Pharaoh's armies, the Israelites lost their proper perspective on the situation. They only saw the enemy's numbers and their own inability. But God gave Moses the vision to lead the people to safety: "Then the LORD said to Moses, "Why are you crying out to me? Tell the Israelites to move on. Raise your staff and stretch out your hand over the sea to divide the water so that the Israelites can go through the sea on dry ground" (Exodus 14:15–16). Moses had already had an experience with God working miraculously through him. Now, it was Moses's turn to lead the Israelites and allow God to work through him.

Many of us have experienced God's power. It takes God's vision to access his power, but first, we must focus on who God is, not on our situation.

LAY DOWN WORLDLY PERSPECTIVE

Elisha's servant needed vision in his life. But not his own vision, God's vision. He needed to perceive his situation, not merely accept reality. Look at 2 Kings 6:15–20:

> When the servant of the man of God got up and went out early the next morning, an army with horses and chariots had surrounded the city. "Oh no, my lord! What shall we do?" the servant asked. "Don't be afraid," the prophet answered. "Those who are with us are more than those who are with them." And Elisha prayed, "Open his eyes, LORD, so that he may see." Then the LORD opened the servant's eyes, and he looked and saw the hills full of horses and chariots of fire all around Elisha.

I SURRENDER ALL (SORT OF) | 97

As soon as the servant saw he was outnumbered by chariots and armies of people prepared to do battle, he became afraid and cried out to Elisha, "Oh no, my lord!" During my most anxious times, all I did—and all I could do when I felt like my world was crumbling around me—was cry out to God. This is the first key to surrendering your vision—cry out to God when you can't see any way out of your situation. Sometimes I cried out to God through the pages of a journal. Other times it was through times of open and honest prayer.

Do you need to be reassured it's OK not to be OK? It is OK to cry out to God for support when you feel overwhelmed by your current situation! You also may not receive a concrete solution for your current struggle. God may not give you vision right away as to how your situation will resolve. Life throws curveballs—trust me, I know that—but we can take it day-by-day, relying on God to reveal his vision in his time. Until he reveals it, trust God that his timing is perfect.

The prophet calmed his servant by reassuring him he was not alone. It was easy for the servant to feel like everyone was against him and his situation was hopeless. How would you feel if you looked out your window and saw your home surrounded by an army who was against you being a Christian? Even in my own, less desperate situation, some days it was easy for me to turn inward and feel hopeless to even fight. During my anxiety battles, I often felt completely unarmed!

PICK UP LOOKING TO GOD FOR REVELATION

Elisha's servant needed to see what God was doing behind the scenes—not just what was physically around him. When God opened his eyes, he saw the Lord fighting for him. He saw the huge array of angelic armies equipped with the armor and weapons to fight on Elisha's behalf. To practice surrender, it is good for us to regularly ask God to fight on our behalf, even in the worst circumstances.

Sometimes we need reassurance that the Lord is fighting for us behind the scenes. We long for God to reveal his plans and his vision for us, but whether we see it yet or not, God always has a vision for our lives—even if we don't have one at the time. Isaiah 55:8–9 says, "'For my thoughts are not your thoughts, neither are your ways my ways,' declares the Lord. 'As the heavens are higher than the earth, so are my ways higher than your ways and my thoughts than your thoughts.'"

We are not alone in our fights, although it may seem that way. God inhabits a realm of space and time that we will never understand. He works on our behalf in the heavenlies in ways we never see. Part of our joy in heaven will be to discover all the things God spared us from on earth and all the ways God fought for us when we were too weak to defeat our enemies on our own.

THE IMPORTANCE OF VISION

Vision is important, but even the disciples had trouble seeing Jesus for who he really was. Let's consider Luke 24:13–18:

> Now that same day two of them were going to a village called Emmaus, about seven miles from Jerusalem. They were talking with each other about everything that had happened. As they talked and discussed these things with each other, Jesus himself came up and walked along with them; but they were kept from recognizing him. He asked them, "What are you discussing together as you walk along? They stood still, their faces downcast. One of them, named Cleopas, asked him, "Are you the only one visiting Jerusalem who does not know the things that have happened there in these days?"

When Jesus walked alongside the disciples, they first thought he was a stranger. They lacked the vision to recognize Jesus. The breaking of bread proved he was the Son of God. Aren't we blessed to know a Savior who not only walks alongside us in our regular days but can also perform such miracles that astonish everyone in his wake? It is only when we see Jesus for who he is that we can recognize the miracles taking place in our lives.

I've been through terrifying storms with torrential rain, hail, and high winds capable of snapping roofs and bringing trees crashing to the ground. At times, I have been caught in storms while driving, when the rain was so severe I pulled over because I couldn't see what was in front of me! In such moments, continuing to drive became too dangerous because I lost vision and focus, so I trusted in God for my safety. Like my vision during a storm, a life without God's vision will easily careen into a ditch if I'm not careful.

A life focused on Christ will always have the vision to stay on course. Taking our eyes off Jesus will only land us into trouble as it did the apostle Peter. Peter was able to imitate Jesus when he kept his eyes on him.

And what was Jesus doing after he sent the disciples into the boat without him? He went up onto a mountainside to pray. He constantly had to renew himself through communing with his Father to do the work—whether miraculous or ordinary—his Father asked of him. He needed to focus on the goal of his earthly work—to give glory to his Father. To do that, he had to see his Father clearly, which he accomplished by focusing on him through prayer.

God loves you. He doesn't want us to go through life with no vision but rather with his vision. We not only need to have proper vision for our own lives, but we can then lead others into discovering God's vision for their lives as well. When we truly surrender, God's people can help us open our eyes, and, like Elisha, see things from his perspective.

Laying It Down

1. In what circumstances of your life do you need to see beyond your own perspective?

2. In what areas of life might vision be difficult to achieve?

3. Why is perspective so important to achieving God's vision for your life?

CHAPTER THIRTEEN—SURRENDER YOUR DISAGREEMENTS

One of the best tips I've ever heard on forgiveness was given during a church service Question and Answer time. Someone asked, "How do you know when you have forgiven someone?"

One woman raised her hand and said, "When you stop talking about it." What a profound statement!

The Scripture, "For the mouth speaks what the heart is full of" (Luke 6:45) fits well here. If we harbor bitterness in our hearts, our mouths will spill out angry statements. The heart is the fuel behind our emotions. Emotions, like the heart, are fickle and can change quickly. When our heart is not in sync with God and wants fleshly things, it gets us into trouble. The heart also drives the mind, which thinks things that then come out of the mouth and eventually lead to action. While it is important for me to renew my mind, the only way to do this is to change my heart. The Israelites were bitter with Moses the moment things looked bleak! This caused them to take out their anger on Moses, but it didn't stop Moses from doing the right thing and leading them to freedom.

LAY DOWN YOUR GRUDGES

I was recently embroiled in a conflict with someone. I held a grudge because I knew I was right and the claims against me were falsehoods. Holding onto my anger was a way to "win" over the person rather than caring about their wellbeing. I had a right to be angry, but as the Lord has dictated, it is our job as Christians to choose peace: "If it is possible, as far as it depends on you, live at peace with everyone "(Romans 12:18).

We will always have conflict. Whether it is in our homes, our schools, or our churches, when we are in relationship with others, conflict is bound to occur. But it matters to God how I react to it. Not only does he call me to forgive the event but also the emotions tied to the incident. Although it may take years to fully forgive a person, as Christians we are obligated to extend the same forgiveness to others that we have received from Christ.

PICK UP FORGIVENESS

Despite this obligation, many of us have some common misconceptions regarding forgiveness:

Many people equate forgiveness or letting something go to forgetting, pretending like the offense never occurred. God himself is a great example of one who forgives but does not forget. Although he is omniscient, God chooses not to remember our sins or hold them against us. This is evident in the parable of the adulterous woman:

> The teachers of the law and the Pharisees brought in a woman caught in adultery. They made her stand before the group and said to Jesus, "Teacher, this woman was caught in the act of adultery. In the Law Moses commanded us to stone such women. Now what do you say?" They were using this question as a trap, to have a basis for accusing him. But Jesus bent down and started to write on the ground with his finger. When they kept on questioning him, he straightened up and said to them, "Let any one of you who is without sin be the first to throw a stone at her." Again, he stooped down and

wrote on the ground. At this, those who heard began to go away one at a time, the older ones first, until only Jesus was left, with the woman still standing there. Jesus straightened up and asked her, "Woman, where are they? Has no one condemned you?" "No one, sir," she said. "Then neither do I condemn you," Jesus declared. "Go now and leave your life of sin." John 8:3–11

A couple of things stand out to me in the above passage:

God does not minimize the sin—We often think if we take the road of grace or mercy, it lets the offender off the hook and allows him not to face the consequences of his sin. This could not be further from the truth since God already paid the penalty of our sin through Christ's death on the cross. To hold someone's sin against him is to think he must pay doubly for the sin that has already been atoned for. To hold a sin against someone is to say, "Christ's death means nothing. It covers some sin but not this one." This minimizes Christ's sacrificial payment for all believers.

Forgiveness frees both the offender and the offended. When we forgive someone, we set ourselves free. That's why forgiveness is so powerful and why Christ's death is so pivotal in our lives as Christians.

While forgiveness is important for us to achieve peace, the reality is, we don't have the power to achieve peace with everyone in this life. But whether others change or not, forgiveness helps us achieve the internal peace we need to live a life of freedom.

As Christ's ambassadors, it is important we lead the world as examples of how to demonstrate Christlike characteristics. These include lavishing mercy and grace on others, forgiving them, and speaking the truth in love to others so they may grow into disciples.

To practice surrender, we can let go of our anger and desire for retaliation. We can have healthy direct conversations face-to-face with those whom we have offended and who have offended us. We can take responsibility for our part in our conflicts. We can express our emotions freely without placing blame, accurately describing the reality of the situation.

Pick Up Judgment

Condemnation and judgment are not the same things. In our pluralistic, individualistic society, we look down on judgment. I often hear Christians say, "Who am I to judge?" Yet, this is our job as Christians. To judge means to declare an act right or wrong according to a law. In our case, we use the Bible to judge an act as right or wrong. Paul tells the Corinthian church:

> I wrote to you in my letter not to associate with sexually immoral people— not at all meaning the people of this world who are immoral, or the greedy and swindlers, or idolaters ... But now I am writing to you that you must not associate with anyone who claims to be a brother or sister but is sexually immoral or greedy, an idolater or slanderer, a drunkard or swindler. Do not even eat with such people. What business is it of mine to judge those outside the church? Are you not to judge those inside? God will judge those outside. "Expel the wicked person from among you" (1 Corinthians 5:9–13)

Judgment is a good thing and has its place within the church, but not condemnation. Judgment says, "We have determined you seem to have done something wrong. I want what is best for you and want to see you at your best. How can I help?" Condemnation says, "You have done something wrong. You're a terrible, awful person and can't come back from it." Scripture has something to say about this: "There is now no condemnation for those who are in Christ Jesus" (Romans 8:1). Jesus paid the penalty for all our sins. There is no sin Christ's death did not atone for.

Think of judgment this way: When conflict involves a legal issue, we take it to court and present our issue before a judge well versed in the law. Lawyers, experts in the law, do their best to argue both sides and try to win the argument by submitting evidence. The person with the most compelling evidence wins the case. We can't always achieve perfect justice here on earth but that doesn't mean we shouldn't fight for justice. We can get close to that justice by being knowledgeable of the law, doing our best to obey it, and allowing judgment to shape us when we do wrong.

Judgment by wise people in our lives helps us see the big picture, especially when we hold a narrow-minded perspective. Here are two reasons why judgment is a good thing:

It helps me to see the error of my ways. It is difficult for me to see my own sin as damaging to my overall wellbeing. For example, King David had engaged in sinful behavior—adultery, murder, etc.—but convinced himself what he was doing was OK. The prophet Nathan spoke truth to him when no one else did. As a result, David repented from his sin, surrendered his pride, and was then able to lead his people effectively.

Judgment makes us more like Christ. Christ calls his church the bride. He desires for his people to be spotless and radiate his beauty upon his return. When we speak the truth into each other's lives, we become better disciples as a result.

Condemnation was overcome at the cross. But judgment helps us make informed decisions that benefit not only our lives but the lives of others too. Judgment is important in church life because, when used effectively, it can help people who may be going astray in the faith reorient themselves to a godlier path.

Sweep Clean Your Soul

Surrender requires us to forgive those who have wronged us, and to do that, we need to make sure we have dealt with the issues that clutter our own soul. I understood this concept in a new way during a routine spring cleaning.

I needed to tackle a huge task: my closet. It had been a mess for a while, and after many months of putting it off, I rolled up my sleeves and got to work. I filled garbage bags with clothes hidden so long I had forgotten I even had them and swept the dirt out. Then I surveyed my work. Tops color coordinated; jeans folded neatly on top of one another. I was especially happy to throw those pieces out that were dusty, old, or stained!

When I was done, I felt something: joy. It took a lot of perseverance to get there, but the thought that my closet would be organized was worth every minute of effort I put into it. It also gave me a sense of relief. I had done the work of cleaning, and now I would reap the rewards of a well-ordered closet.

When I woke up next morning, I still felt weighed down, just in a different way, as a church conflict reared its ugly head. Suddenly, unresolved emotions from past betrayals emerged as if they had been on the surface all along. I realized I hadn't dealt effectively with everything. I knew I *had* to forgive, but I didn't *feel* like it. And little by little, that unwillingness crept into my soul and cluttered it, much like the excess of all those cute skirts and tops.

Lysa Terkeurst in her book *Forgiving What You Can't Forget* shared an exercise her counselor had her do while Lysa was reeling from her husband's betrayal. He asked her to write out on index cards each offense her husband had committed against her. Then she spoke out each offense with this statement, "I choose to forgive _____ for

I SURRENDER ALL (SORT OF) | 107

_____. And whatever my feelings can't catch up to, the blood of Christ will cover." She states she felt a weight lifted off her. How nice it must have felt to have her soul swept clean.[1]

Just like my closet, my soul needed to be purged and swept clean too. So, I did what Lysa did. I filled my journal with words so strong all my emotions poured out on the page. I prayed and cried out to God, racked with sobs so powerful I thought my insides would fall out. But I did the backbreaking, gut-wrenching work my soul needed, and I came out of it with the emotional and mental freedom a child of God deserves. I wanted to experience the fullness of a life free from anger and sadness. I also believed I was worth the love of Christ and, to eagerly extend full forgiveness, I had to make sure my soul was free of vengeance and the need for retaliation.

Pick Up Freedom

How about you? What is the condition of your soul? Is your soul cluttered, weighed down by the emotional baggage that comes from bad circumstances or the hindrances of life? Or do you wake up feeling free, full of the joy afforded to you by Jesus Christ? If you need to sweep clean your soul, try some of these strategies:

Examine your heart. Is there unconfessed sin, unforgiveness, anger, or bitterness keeping you from being free? Journal your feelings and the events tied to these feelings. If you aren't sure what might be making you feel angry or bitter, ask the Holy Spirit. He is our advocate whose primary role is to comfort and convict. Enlist his help.

Name the offense. Speak out the offense using Lysa's statement outlined above. Don't make a blanket statement, clumping all offenses together. Turn each offense over to God individually. By doing so, you take away its power.

Declare the truth. We often forget the authority Jesus gave to each of his disciples: "I have given you authority to trample on snakes and scorpions and to overcome all the power of the enemy; nothing will harm you" (Luke 10:19). Use your voice and declare the truth.

When we acknowledge our authority given to us in Jesus, we experience freedom like never before. We no longer have to be enslaved to others' opinions or Satan's schemes. Tell Satan where he truly belongs. Declare your home and church a place where the Holy Spirit is welcomed and where Satan is ousted. This is the authority we have the privilege of walking in every day. Let's not forget where (and to whom) we belong.

Soul sweeping is tough. But the freedom and joy you gain is well worth the time and effort.

Bless Those Who Curse You

Conflict is unavoidable. In our ministry, my husband and I have faced our fair share of conflict, even in the church. At a former church, members spread gossip about my husband and me, ruining our reputation not only in our community but with our leadership team as well. People who we thought were friends became our enemies.

I felt like I was walking to the guillotine to be executed the day I walked into a meeting to confront our accusers. Why do people in the ministry get treated this way? I thought. Insults were hurled; accusations were made; feelings were hurt. After a hostile meeting, we and our accusers parted ways, but not amicably. Myriad emotions stung my psyche. Hurt. Betrayal. Anger.

They were supposed to be our friends. How could they do this to us?

As time went on, a new set of emotions emerged. Bitterness. Resentment. Rage. I was hesitant to forgive and reluctant to trust anyone again.

As I reflected on my feelings, God reminded me of this passage in Luke 6:27–28: "But to you who are listening I say: Love your enemies, do good to those who hate you, bless those who curse you, pray for those who mistreat you." My friends had become my enemies, but that didn't mean they had to stay that way.

After reading those verses, I knew I had the best weapon of all—the gift of blessing. Satan was trying to steal my joy, but I wasn't going to let him get away with it. As God always does, he allows us to take part in the redemptive work he is doing in the lives of his children, thwarting Satan's plans to seek vengeance. This meant instead of seeking retaliation, I could seek to bless those who curse me.

Easier said than done.

I presented myself with a challenge. For one week, I would pray a prayer of blessing over my enemies in the hopes that it would not only change my perspective on the situation but also my heart. Initially, I resisted forgiveness because I didn't want to let my offenders off the hook. But even though I didn't feel like forgiving, I knew my act of obedience would not only set me free but would also bring glory to God. I sat in my chair and spoke this prayer aloud:

"Lord, please bless _____. I know he/she is my enemy right now, but please bring your healing to the situation. Turn our turmoil into peace, our sorrow into joy, and our despair into hope."

On Monday, the words were like eating sour lemons—downright unpleasant. By Wednesday, they came a bit more naturally. *By Friday, they tasted sweet like honey.*

Praying a prayer of blessing over my enemies was a tall order. When I think about the situation, it still brings up feelings of anger and betrayal. Yet Jesus afforded me the gift of forgiveness with his death on the cross. I didn't have to forgive in my own strength but rather through Christ's strength. If he can bless his enemies then so can I. This process is worth the effort because blessing someone who hates me makes me love them even more. *Every time I do it, something within me changes.* My character becomes more like Jesus. The words become less bitter and a little sweeter. My thoughts are a little less angry and a little more peaceful.

I hope the next time I have something to forgive and need to utter those words, I won't have to think twice about them. I hope they will roll off my tongue with ease. Like Proverbs 16:24 says, "Gracious words are a honeycomb, sweet to the soul and healing to the bones."

And my soul is feeling pretty clean right now.

LAYING IT DOWN

1. What is the difference between condemnation and judgment?

2. Why is it important for the church to judge those inside the church (to judge means to declare an action morally right or wrong based on the Bible)?

3. Take a moment to examine your heart. Who do you need to forgive? Make a list then practice the exercise outlined above. How do you feel about your offender after a week of doing this?

CHAPTER FOURTEEN—SURRENDER YOUR MARRIAGE

Anyone who has been married for any length of time knows how difficult it can be. Married for twenty-one years as I write this, my husband and I have had our ups and downs. In the fall of 2019, during my bout with anxiety, we experienced a breaking point. We took our stressors out on each other, creating a less-than-ideal situation. But during COVID-19, as we spent so much time together, we began to realize something—if we were going to have a successful marriage, we were going to have to face the issues plaguing our souls and our marriage. We may not have liked the package it came in, but sometimes gifts come in rough and bumpy packages, like hard conversations.

LAY DOWN SELFISHNESS

Christ is meant to be at the center of every relationship. This is especially true of marriage since it is a mirror of Christ in the church. We, as the church, are his bride and he will one day return for us. The way we love our spouses demonstrates to the world God's love for us. Ephesians 5:25–27 says, "Husbands, love your wives, just as Christ loved the church and gave himself up for her to make her holy, cleansing her by the washing with water through the word, and to present her to himself as a radiant church, without stain or wrinkle or any other blemish, but holy and blameless."

Sadly, the church is rife with divorce and other sins that rob it of the opportunity to be a good example of Christlike qualities that represent God to the world. While we can't change our whole culture, we can change the dynamics in our own marriages.

If we are honest with ourselves, our marriage problems are rooted in one area—selfishness. When we don't put our spouse first every day, we begin to look inward. We begin to focus only on our needs, wants, and desires instead of sacrificing ourselves for our spouse. Surrendering to God leads us to treat our mates with attitudes that reflect the fruit of the Spirit."

LAY DOWN YOUR DREAMS

My friend Melanie Coleman knows this all too well when she had to surrender her marriage:

> I didn't have my first serious relationship until I was twenty-nine, and we dated for a year before marrying. I met him through a church group, and he seemed solid—he had close communication with his family and attended church autonomously as an adult. We had a few speed bumps during the engagement, but we got married in a big ceremony, nonetheless. I knew from early in the relationship that he was sober, but because I had little to no experience with alcoholism, I didn't see any warning signs leading up to the wedding.
>
> Throughout the entire first year of our marriage, he drank in front of me, but also hid large amounts of alcohol in his office, often passing out in there. I also found he had a deep and systemic addiction to pornography, which kept any hope of emotional and physical intimacy far away. He also became very verbally abusive and emotionally manipulative—I found myself cowering in a corner while he yelled at me most

evenings, and then his guilt would consume him, and I had to switch immediately from traumatized victim to trusted counselor and rescuer for my abuser.

We hit a critical mass in the days leading up to our first wedding anniversary, and the day before, he finally hit a rock bottom and agreed to residential rehab. I took him there, and spent our first anniversary home alone, crying over a bowl of cereal that night. He came home a month later, and after the initial novelty of sobriety wore off, the abuse reached new heights as he felt the pain of his problems without the aid of alcohol. Pornography seemed to take over his life. About ten months later, he relapsed. That night, he solicited sexual pictures and favors from another woman and when I took our dog out to ensure its care for the evening, in his anger he took a hammer to our house, smashing everything that I owned and destroying the walls. I never slept in my home again after that night.

I spent days upon days praying to God, asking him why he gave me this marriage if it was going to fail. "How am I supposed to do this? How are we supposed to come back from this? Is my husband right? Am I as much to blame as he is? How do I fix it?" I cried countless tears as I desperately tried to control the situation and navigate our lives back to safety, but nothing I tried worked. I struggled valiantly to reclaim our marriage and get back to what I believe God intended, but instead, our marriage seemed to dissolve further. Every effort I made could not stop this decay, no matter how intensely I fought.

One night as I lay in bed in my parent's home, exhausted, I gave up. I admitted to God, through a haze of tears, that I could not do this anymore. I couldn't save my husband or our marriage. Instead of waiting for God to tell me how to do what I wanted, and thought was needed, I finally gave it all right to him. For the first time, I surrendered my expectations and released my white knuckles from the future that was "supposed to be," and gave God the space he had been waiting for, to enter this situation and begin healing me.

For the first time in years, I felt true peace—a peace I could not understand. The relief overwhelmed me, and it took some days of living in this new surrendered state before my next steps became clear.

Now free from my own expectations and released from the fear of failure through divorce, I met again with counsel. This time, God showed me clearly the path he made for me to move forward. I knew God was grieved by the necessity of divorce, and I grieved deeply as well. I continued to surrender every day in the divorce process, and as PTSD threatened to overtake me, it was only by routinely meeting with God and laying all these things at his feet that I began to process and heal.[1]

"Do not be yoked together with unbelievers. For what do righteousness and wickedness have in common? Or what fellowship can light have with darkness?" (2 Corinthians 6:14). While Scripture is clear we should not be unequally yoked with unbelievers, what does this mean for those yoked with a believer who is not as mature spiritually? I can do my best in my marriage to honor my spouse, but I am ultimately responsible for my growth in God. I can do my best to choose someone dedicated to Jesus, but there is no guarantee they will remain on that same path.

When I am yoked with someone who is not moving in the same direction as me, I am tempted to allow my situation to stunt my growth in the Lord. If you are in a relationship with an unbeliever, count the cost as to what that might mean for your spiritual growth in the years ahead. You may think you can change your partner, but that rarely occurs. Consider what it will be like to raise children in the faith with an unbeliever who may change their mind and disagree about having your children raised in your faith—they now want the children to be able to choose. While it is important to have a partner who is smart, caring, and generous, the most important quality of a partner is one who wants to walk every day in unity and in step with you and the Lord.

PICK UP SACRIFICE

Marriage takes work, not only work on our marriage but also work on ourselves. It is only when we allow God to work on our souls that we can be the best version of ourselves to our spouses. Galatians 5:22–25 says, "But the fruit of the Spirit is love, joy, peace, forbearance, kindness, goodness, faithfulness, gentleness, and self-control. Against such things there is no law. Those who belong to Christ Jesus have crucified the flesh with its passions and desires. Since we live by the Spirit, let us keep in step with the Spirit."

Walking with the Spirit means to walk in the way of love. Imagine taking each step of the day as a sacrificial act of worship to the Savior. Ephesians 6:7–8 says, "Serve wholeheartedly, as if you were serving the Lord, not people, because you know that the Lord will reward each one for whatever good they do, whether they are slave or free." We can demonstrate the love of Christ in the small and the big acts. Every time we perform a menial task—making the bed, doing the dishes, sweeping the floor—for our spouse, it's an act of worship to God.

Since marriage mirrors Christ's relationship to the church, let's consider the people in your local church. It is easy to make people believe you are close to God by reciting Bible verses, praying with grandiose words, and attending church and serving. But what about those who make the sacrifice behind the scenes? What about the person who comes to church an hour earlier than everyone to set up coffee and make sure the bulletins are in the proper place and every chair is exactly in the row as it should be? We know the higher places on the altar—preaching, worship, and other leadership positions get their rewards every

Sunday. But what about the janitor, the usher, or the person washing dishes after the monthly potluck? It's the same in our marriage. Each partner must make sacrifices for the other. It takes sacrifice to do a load of dishes and cleaning even after a long day at work when it's easier to leave it to the spouse who normally does them. These are small sacrifices, but we can also make big sacrifices too. What about the spouse who quits his job to care for the children? Or the spouse who allows the other to take a pay cut to pursue a dream job?

Step-by-step, the Spirit asks us to do the next loving thing in sacrifice to our spouse. As a wife, I can write a note to my husband every morning describing his admirable character traits. I know this is important to him and I can intentionally choose to make this a part of my routine. I can voluntarily take on menial tasks around the house without complaining that it's not my job. I can think to shut off the TV and spend an hour talking or listening to his day, without expecting him to ask me about my day. The opportunities to bless my spouse sacrificially are endless!

Our spouses are not there for our gratification but for our transformation. When we can put our spouses before ourselves, we remind the world of the ultimate sacrificial love of Jesus here on earth. Both small and big sacrifices can have great meaning in a marriage if done in love rather than out of obligation or force.

Just as marriage is the mirror of Jesus the sacrificial lamb who atoned for our sins, we must live our lives in daily sacrifice to each other. Writer and speaker Nancy C. Anderson learned about how to be Jesus to her husband in her marriage when she surrendered to her husband's forgiveness and let go of the shame and regret of having an affair:

> The shame of past pleasures followed me. Eventually though, I came to see that I would have to surrender to forgiveness

to free myself from the prison. God and my husband had already given me the keys, but I had refused to use them. Finally, one day, I did.

I found victory through surrender as I prayed, "Lord, I give up. I cannot carry this anymore. I know that you have forgiven me and so has Ron, and today I choose to receive that forgiveness. Now I ask you for strength as I let go of the guilt, the shame, the sorrow, and I choose to walk toward your light. You have set me free, so I am free indeed." I refused to entertain the stray thoughts anymore. Instead, I replaced them with images of the new life that Ron and I were building. I memorized Philippians 4:8 and only thought about things that were true, lovely, and virtuous. I also discovered that encouraging others with our story of restoration gave a purpose to our pain. This summer, twenty-seven years after my affair, we will celebrate our thirtieth wedding anniversary and our marriage is strong, loving, and healed.[2]

No matter what I'm going through, I can be Jesus in my marriage to my spouse. The union of one man and one woman demonstrates God's union of both male and female: "So, God created mankind in his own image, in the image of God he created them; male and female he created them" (Genesis 1:27). Every time I treat my spouse with attributes of the Spirit and with love, I am showing the world who Jesus is, and I am using my marriage as an opportunity to worship Jesus.

LAYING IT DOWN

1. In what areas can you surrender your marriage to God?

2. In what areas do you display selfishness toward your spouse?

3. How has your perspective about your marriage being a mirror of Christ's love to your spouse changed because of reading this chapter?

4. What can you do to be a better mirror of Christ to your spouse?

CHAPTER FIFTEEN—SURRENDER YOUR CHILDREN'S IDENTITIES

A few months after our move to a new town in Pennsylvania, our fifteen-year-old daughter, a natural extrovert, became withdrawn and not the happy kid of just a few months prior. As we talked with her, I started to notice she wasn't making many new friends.

"I don't have any close relationships, Mom," she confessed. "It's hard to make friends," I responded.

As we talked, she listened to her music. "Whatcha listening to?"

"One of my favorite bands." She had developed an obsession with music from obscure bands and had been listening to this music for some time (no surprise here; I can neither confirm nor deny I have a collection of over 700 records of '80s music.) I asked her what she liked about them. "They are unique and although they are famous, they often feel alone, like no one understands them. They make music I can relate to."

Finally, the lightbulb in my head came on.

"Is it possible," I asked, "that the reason why you really like this music is because you and the bands both feel alone, and your lack of connection makes you feel lonely?" She broke down and sobbed, and I cried with her. "I'm so sorry. Because you really are a fabulous young woman and people are missing out on your friendship."

Lay Down Conditional Love

What we spend our time consuming we relate to more closely than we realize. Months after we talked, my daughter perked up. Although I believed she was doing OK, one Saturday a few months later, we talked again. As a typical teenager, she first groused about doing chores and other normal teenage angst about not having parents that listen, etc. However, she began to talk about this sudden need to be perfect or to be a "good pastor's kid." This confused me because we have never put our kids under strict guidelines or rules about being perfect in the church's eyes.

As she spoke, I began to get suspicious that perhaps she was hiding something from us. After a while of talking to her, I asked to see her phone. We allowed her to have a phone but with rules regarding what social media apps she could use, what places she could go online, etc. This included looking at text messages to see whom she was chatting with and what types of messages were being exchanged. When we looked through her phone, we found inappropriate topics of conversation. This broke my husband and me. We had never put rules on being perfect, but we did expect she was spiritually mature enough to be able to discern good from bad content.

This led to many long talks in our home and stricter monitoring of our daughter's phone and computer. It also led to a deeper look into Scripture to get to the heart of why she would be talking in inappropriate ways. I shut down her computer and took away her phone, but as Christians, I needed to get a hold of her heart. Although we can never change someone's heart for them, an important part of parenting is teaching our children to get to the root of why behaviors are taking place. As I talked with her, we quickly realized she was struggling with her identity and her overall feelings of worth and value. Isn't that also what so many of us struggle with? We struggle with wanting the approval *of others rather* than the approval of God.

That is what we wanted our daughter to understand. We wanted her to walk away from our conversations with an identity rooted in God's love for her. We got out the Bible and reviewed verses that spoke specifically about who she was in God's eyes. We also reassured her we would love her no matter what she did in life and our love was unconditional. She didn't have to prove herself to us or anyone else—she only needed to be who God wanted her to be. We wanted her to know that as a daughter of the King she was already royalty!

PICK UP GRACE

Grace is what the prodigal son parable in Luke teaches us. Previously, we looked at this passage from the eldest brother's perspective. But in this chapter, let's look at the same passage from the prodigal son's viewpoint:

> But while he was still a long way off, his father saw him and was filled with compassion for him; he ran to his son, threw his arms around him and kissed him. The son said to him, "Father, I have sinned against heaven and against you. I am no longer worthy to be called your son." But the father said to his servants, "Quick! Bring the best robe and put it on him. Put a ring on his finger and sandals on his feet. Bring the fattened calf and kill it. Let's have a feast and celebrate. For this son of mine was dead and is alive again; he was lost and is found." So they began to celebrate.

His father still loved the prodigal son, regardless of what he had done. He didn't have to prove his worth. While part of his lostness was the lifestyle he was living—the other part was not understanding his father's unconditional love. It was the father's grace that made him worthy. Nothing he did could change the father's love for him. And it doesn't change God's love for us either.

The Israelites at the Red Sea experienced this unconditional love. God could have punished them right then for their complaining and grumbling against Moses. But he chose to save them. Haven't we all experienced the saving grace of God despite the times when we don't deserve it?

When we submit to God, we don't have to prove ourselves to anyone. First Corinthians 4:3 says, "I care very little if I am judged by you or by any human court; indeed, I do not even judge myself." God's grace is sufficient by Jesus's death on the cross. The key at the heart of surrender is grace. My identity is not rooted in things like having perfect children or a good marriage. It is about chasing after the holiness of God, being sanctified in his presence.

This is a part of the freedom of living a life of surrender. It is allowing ourselves permission to not have to prove ourselves to anyone. We never want to make someone else feel like they have to be inferior to us and we never feel the need to be superior either.

Isn't that freeing?

While we were worried for our daughter, we had to let go of having a daughter who wholeheartedly followed the Lord. In that moment, we realized she was no longer a little girl, but a young woman who had a mind and will of her own. During a tough conversation, I told her she was free to make the choice to accept Christianity or not: "I can only do my part to be the best parent possible and love you unconditionally," I said. "But it's your choice if you want to follow God or not." Those were some of the hardest words I have ever said. But as I have learned about surrender, I have come to the end of myself, given up control, and let God have his way in her life.

Fast forward a year. I approached her about reading the Bible together, and she was willing to have weekly meetings with me. We talk about what we found interesting or questioned about that week's reading or what we could apply to our lives today. Meetings often end in laughter or deep conversation about the hot button topics in today's world. At the end of one study, she said, "I love this study. It's cool." She also added she had started a Bible study with two friends from her youth group where they reviewed books of the Bible.

My point is this: I wanted my daughter to live free. Free in her life in Christ. Free as a daughter of the King. Free to know him and not feel like she had to perform or be perfect in any way. I also wanted her to know her father and I loved her regardless of what she had done (or not done.) She had to come to her own conclusions regarding faith, God, and life.

Praise God who allows us to be free so we can freely choose him.

LAYING IT DOWN

1. Teens are hard to surrender. How can you surrender them to God, yet still guide and direct them?

2. Do you struggle with conditional love in your relationship with your children? How does your understanding of grace change your view of them?

3. How do you handle it when your kids make a bad choice? How can you show them the love of Christ through that difficulty?

CHAPTER SIXTEEN—SURRENDER YOUR FINANCES

"As a writer, you won't make much money."

Being a certified writing coach, I hate to burst my clients' bubbles about the amount of money they can make as a writer. Yet, it's the sad reality of the business that I don't make much money for what I do. I work hard, grasping at whatever chunk of time I can to get those precious words to paper. Then I edit the manuscript, design the cover, create a marketing plan, and wait—for someone, anyone, to love my work. That's when the aspect of money comes into play. I love what I do, but if I don't make any money for it, is it even worth it?

Many of us want to make money in our careers. However, money is more than just a paycheck; it has more significance than that. Money makes our work valuable and more than just a hobby. At times we may choose to donate our time and effort, but we still want to feel like our work matters.

Lay Down Earthly Wealth

Growing up, I learned early on that my work had to have a paycheck attached to it. When I talk to my father, he asks me, "Don't you remember me working ninety hours a week?" My dad worked hard to put food on our table. My mother, a stay-at-home mom, took care of me and my sister. As a one-income home, we had enough for necessities, but not much for frivolities. My mother also shaped my view of money because of her childhood. She grew up right after the Depression and was so poor her family would sometimes go to a funeral and then to the bereaved family's home just to get a free meal. We never ate out, rarely took vacations, never spent money foolishly. My family always had the basics, but we didn't have a lot of fun in life and took life more seriously than was necessary.

This gave me an unhealthy view of money. I have never made much income. Whether I was working as a director at a daycare or writing, money has always been tight. When my husband and I planted our church, money became even tighter. I began to think I needed a paycheck (even if it's small) to be attached to what I do so my work would have value in others' eyes.

The American Dream plays into this erroneous thinking. This idea dictates we must work to have worth and value. But money is often disproportionate to the value of work. Teachers and nurses make basic wages saving lives, while celebrities make tons of money just by being beautiful. When we don't earn income for what we do, we can feel worthless, like our work doesn't matter.

Yet, there is an eternal significance to whatever we do. I am convinced part of our joy in heaven will be hearing from and meeting people who have experienced our impact whom we never had any contact with here on earth. I surrender my earthly wealth to God so my eternal significance can pay dividends in heaven. Hearing stories of how we have made a difference in their lives is more of a paycheck to me than money. But while I long to earn more of these eternal rewards, I also have to focus on everyday things like putting food on my table and keeping the lights on in my home.

When we planted a church from 2007 to 2012, it strained every aspect of our lives, including our marriage and finances. We had to take two pay cuts in a state that was expensive and typically required two full-time incomes just to make ends meet. I hated my daycare job. However, writing doesn't make much money, so I was stuck in a dead-end job torn between doing what made money and doing what I loved.

At the same time, my parents' unhealthy attachment to money and work had become a deeply engrained lie that to be worthy in life, I must work and make money. I unconsciously assumed this was part of my intrinsic value—my identity—that at the core of who I am, I must work to make money.

Even after that hard time, my motivation to make money to prove my worth and value still prevented me from walking in freedom, not only in my writing career but also in my walk with God.

One day, my husband and I went to our church for a morning of personal prayer. We both felt strongly we needed to pray over our church, so it could reap the benefits of growth and health. As we began, we prayed over the church building, the members, the chairs, and each section of the sanctuary. We asked the Holy Spirit what he wanted us to pray for. My husband felt prompted to read from Joel 2:28–29 that says, "And afterward, I will pour out my Spirit on all people. Your sons and daughters will prophesy, your old men will dream dreams, your young men will see visions. Even on my servants, both men and women, I will pour out my Spirit in those days."

When I heard that verse in Joel, I felt like God was saying I needed to let go of my attachment to earning money. When I told my husband, he reassured me he didn't need me to make money. He has never told me I needed to make money and, except for that brief church planting time, has always done an excellent job of providing for me and our children. But because I believed a lie that my work was not valuable without a paycheck, I often worked under the wrong motivations.

During that time of prayer, I experienced a release from an unhealthy attachment to earning money. I am grateful to be in a place financially where I don't have to have a full-time income apart from my writing to make ends meet. But if you must have an income, be encouraged.

My friend Meg W. from Coudersport, Pennsylvania, shared her story about the difficulty of laying down her finances and trusting in God:

> It was Ramadan and we were living in the United Arab Emirates. As I watched my Muslim friends fast, their demeanor and attitudes changed. Physically, they looked healthier and serene, like they were glowing. I thought I needed serenity and closeness with God, so I looked up fasting for Christians and found the Daniel Fast.
>
> I asked my pastor's wife about it, and she said, "Meg, you have to do it! It's so amazing but watch out for day seven. Things get crazy!" I wanted to know more, and it turns out she and her husband had been unable to have children for many years. They got pregnant on day seven! Miracle of miracles!
>
> I went home, prayed, and started the Daniel Fast then shared my fasting with my Muslim friends. We talked about how God changed our hearts while doing so, and I was praying for discernment on what to do next with our lives. I really liked Dubai, and we were building a home. Our daughter was in preschool and doing well. We had a church, friends, and jobs.
>
> Then, day seven came. My husband found out that his workplace was not renewing his contract, and I was let go from my position where I worked. Immediately, Tim wanted to pack our bags and go home because if we went into debt

there, the law says we would go to prison. Obviously, he didn't want to go to prison in the Middle East.

For some reason, I couldn't leave. I felt God wanted us to stay, and I was at peace and needed to see things through according to my morals. We weren't leaving in the dark of night because we would no longer be able to pay our bills. Additionally, my employer had taken my passport to remove the visa. I felt the Holy Spirit prompting me to stay. We didn't have enough money to get home, and there were certain things and people I wasn't just ready to abandon.

Fast forward to day ten: my former employer bought all three of us tickets home and paid for our luggage. My Pakistani landlord let us out of our lease early—something totally unheard of there. Rhiannon's preschool refunded her tuition; again, something that does not occur. The martial arts school I went to refunded all my tuition, another miracle. On my last day at the office, all my colleagues chipped in together and handed me an envelope full of cash with more than $3,000. What a blessing! God answered!

In addition, the tenants of our house back home were moving out. We could go back to our very first home! Also, my husband's photography business started receiving inquiries about photoshoots as soon as we were able to return. In the end, we were able to leave the country with dignity, with our bills paid, with hugs from friends, and hope for the future. We were even able to buy a car with cash! God was so good to us! God is good.[1]

Just because you need a paycheck to meet your physical needs does not mean you need a paycheck to meet your soul's needs.

Pick Up True Value

We are all motivated by something. Either we are motivated by things like a desire for wealth and fame or we are motivated by working out of a place of purpose. All our motivations come down to two factors:

Intrinsic values—the overarching beliefs that make up the core of who you are. My intrinsic values are honesty and integrity. These coincide with the godly character God wants for me. Such values shape who I am. I do my best to operate within these values. When I am in conflict and someone questions my integrity, it causes me to strongly react because their words are going against my intrinsic values.

Expressed values—the behaviors that I engage in as a result of my intrinsic values. For example, since honesty is my intrinsic value, I do my best to behave in a way that allows me to live with integrity the best I possibly can with others. Integrity is important in my finances because I choose to do the right things with money and not squander or spend it unwisely.

Extravagant living can be an expressed value based on a belief that you have to have fancy things to be valuable, but this will cause you to live above your means. When we see ourselves as valuable just because God says so, we are free to see how our work and money can have an eternal value—the most important value of all—because of the difference we make in others' lives.

Debora Coty, best-selling author of the *Too Blessed to Be Stressed* book series, surrendered her job for the sake of another coworker because of her intrinsic value of always honoring others and God:

> The choice came down to this: Nancy or me. One of us would lose our job. And as her supervisor, the call was mine.
>
> The thing was, Nancy *needed* her job. She was the sole supporter of her household of three, although she didn't make all that much as a Certified Occupational Therapy Assistant (COTA). Still, it was enough to keep her driving forty miles per day in a rickety old jalopy across a long Tampa Bay bridge through rain, shine, or wind-gusting hurricane,

I SURRENDER ALL (SORT OF) | 133

for the six years since I had hired her as my assistant at a skilled nursing facility/rehab center.

But I needed my job too. My position as a part-time Registered Occupational Therapist (OTR) enabled me to be a hands-on mother to my two young children while keeping a roof over our heads and food on the table for my growing family. My husband's income alone was simply not enough.

I'd heard snippets from facility administration for several months about burgeoning discontent with Nancy's job performance. She did tend to be a bit distracted, especially during the hours I was not there to directly supervise, and her New England bluntness grated many Southern nerves. It was no wonder she had few close friends, and her coworkers often rolled their eyes behind her back.

But my relationship with Nancy seemed preordained. Since I was a small child, Papa God blessed me with the gift of acceptance. It's been my privilege to be able to overlook the annoying faults of many socially outcast acquaintances and love them as cherished friends.

Over the years we worked together, Nancy had become like family to me. My kids called her Aunt Nancy. She was a guest in our home often, and it had become tradition for her to spend a day at Christmastime celebrating the birth of our Savior with us.

How could I just sit back and let circumstances deteriorate to the point of her being fired? It would demoralize her spirit. And crush her family.

Yet if she left voluntarily for another job, I realized my own hard-won job was at risk. They would no doubt want me to increase my hours to full time so they wouldn't have to hire a replacement for Nancy. I felt convicted that my preschool children needed me at this crucial time of their lives, and that I needed to remain part time. But part-time OT jobs were extremely difficult to find. I would likely be out in the cold.

What to do? Time was of the essence. Pressure felt smothering. I agonized over the decision. I could hardly sleep or eat. I prayed. And prayed some more. Then I found my answer: "Trust in the LORD with all your heart and lean not on your own understanding; in all your ways submit to him, and he will make your paths straight" (Proverbs 3:5–6).

When I surrendered my future to the Lord, the decision made itself. I would take the risk of losing my job. The one who held the future in his hands would take care of me. I felt Papa God's supernatural peace warm my heart. I knew it was the right thing to do, whatever the outcome. But helping Nancy through the transition to a new job would be tricky. She'd had a lot of devastating rejection in her life and could scarcely handle more.

To spare her feelings and fragile self-esteem, I began quietly urging Nancy to look for job openings nearer to her home, pointing out that it would make her commute so much shorter. I painted a picture of an exciting new beginning and offered to write her a letter of recommendation. I even located several posted positions for which she was qualified and encouraged her to go for interviews.

Papa God blessed those efforts, and within a matter of weeks, Nancy was offered a COTA position within fifteen minutes of her house. She was thrilled to be wanted. She never noticed our administrator's sigh of relief when she turned in her resignation (days before he was going to let her go) and left for her new job with her head held high and dignity intact (she ended up happily employed by that company for the next fifteen years.)

A week later, I lost my job.

The administrator called me into his office and all but begged me to come on full-time, but I knew I couldn't. So, two months after Nancy left, so did I. It wasn't unexpected. I'd known in my heart all along that it was inevitable, but I daily re-surrendered my future to the Lord and leaned on my trust in him.

And true to his promise, Papa God provided. Out of the blue, a good friend-therapist decided to start her own rehab company and hired me as her first employee. It turned out to be one of the best positions I've ever had—a decent paying, part-time job with flexible hours that met my family's needs and was great fun to boot!²

LAYING IT DOWN

1. Do you find yourself attaching your value and worth to your paycheck? How can this be a hazard to your spiritual and emotional health?

2. How can you use your money and resources to meet others' needs rather than shape your identity?

3. Can you see how living within your means is a way of surrendering to God?

CHAPTER SEVENTEEN—SURRENDER YOUR WORK

"Your work is unusable."

That was tough to hear. As a writer, every book that I write is like a baby to me. I put my heart and soul into each book I write, so when someone criticizes my work, I can easily take it personally and get offended. This was no exception.

I was connected to someone who needed help with editing and other writing projects. I enjoyed the work and was able to use my skills to polish her writing, so I was happy when I received a phone call one evening to invite me to do a ghostwriting project for her. The biggest hurdle—she wanted the book in six days! I knew no quality work could be done within that time, but I worked all weekend talking to her, transcribed the phone calls, and created an edited manuscript. I sent my work to her, and she initially approved the work. But as the weeks wore on, it was clear we were not a good fit. When a disagreement turned into an attack on my work, I had no choice but to stop working for her.

When we live a life of surrender, we lay down every aspect of our lives, including our work. We may spend the majority of our waking time at our workplaces, but even there, they can be the places where we make the most impact for the kingdom.

Lay Down Useless Labor

Previously in this book, we talked about work being a part of paradise. But in Genesis 3 everything changed:

> To Adam he said, "Because you listened to your wife and ate fruit from the tree about which I commanded you, 'You must not eat from it,' Cursed is the ground because of you; through painful toil you will eat food from it all the days of your life. It will produce thorns and thistles for you, and you will eat the plants of the field. By the sweat of your brow you will eat your food until you return to the ground, since from it you were taken; for dust you are and to dust you will return." Genesis 3:17–19

Because of the fall, work is laborious, often leaving us exhausted physically, emotionally, and mentally at the end of the work week. Whether we love our work or not, it can tax us in every way. Since work can take up most of our time per week, it can consume our minds and ultimately our lives if we don't learn to carefully prioritize it.

Judy Douglass was hired to be a part of Campus Crusade for Christ, but she had to surrender her work dreams to follow God's calling:

> When I came to Christ at age fifteen at a Young Life camp, I knew little about walking with God. This I was sure of: I was committed to choosing God's way for my life, not my own. And I had an assurance that God had something he wanted me to do. I was called for life.
>
> I remember well when God called me to student staff with Campus Crusade (Cru). In one week both the national women's leader and Bill Bright challenged me to consider joining the staff team at the University of Texas for my junior and senior years. It was an easy yes for me. What a privilege!
>
> Two years later, as I was graduating, I clearly heard the Lord calling me to full time with our ministry. My heart was

eager to say yes, but I had two significant obstacles. My first obstacle was I was engaged. The second obstacle was equally daunting. Ever since I was eight years old, I had wanted to be a writer. As I studied journalism, my dream was refined to a desire to be a magazine writer and editor. At that time, the only thing to do on staff was to go on campus and disciple women. I gave up my dream and said, "Yes, Lord." God had called, asking me to give up my dream to write.

But God had surprises ahead. At staff training, Bill Bright called me into his office. He asked if I would consider coming to Arrowhead Springs to work on the *Collegiate Challenge* evangelistic magazine the ministry was producing. I could have my dream and serve God with the ministry I had come to love? For the next fourteen years, I lived my dream, with far more meaning, purpose, and possibility than I could have asked for or imagined. Nor could I have imagined the following thirty-seven years of opportunity and blessing as well.[1]

Like Judy, God often calls us to give up work that suits the world's goals of money and status for his kingdom work. Even if things don't work out as clearly as they did for Judy, if we surrender to God, our work can be both laborious and also give us great joy.

Pick up Joy and Worship

"Consider it pure joy, my brothers and sisters, whenever you face trials of many kinds, because you know that the testing of your faith produces perseverance. Let perseverance finish its work so that you may be mature and complete, not lacking anything" (James 1:2–4). Joy is a part of our overall purpose. We can treat work like a jail sentence, or we can love what we do because work is a part of our purpose given to us by God.

Work comes in many forms whether we work outside the home or are stay-at-home moms. We are called to be a steward of what God has given us, whether maintaining our homes or caring for our children. It takes work to maintain and grow in our relationships with others, whether it's our marriages or our friends. Some of these take less work, but all require our time and attention on a regular basis. I have often felt like work was a chore or a boring waste of time. But God says I can have joy when I work. First Corinthians 10:31 says, "So whether you eat or drink or whatever you do, do it all for the glory of God."

Have you ever seen work as a gift from God, and doing it well as an act of worship? The ultimate purpose of work is to worship God and give him the glory. Even the smallest of tasks honor God when done with this purpose in mind. I often remind myself of this verse when I'm folding a mountain of clothes or doing a pile of dishes.

Our work can shine a light on God so people can see him better. It can be a living example of Jesus and we can use it to share the good news we have found whether at our jobs, our homes, or our communities. Acts 1:8 says, "But you will receive power when the Holy Spirit comes on you; and you will be my witnesses in Jerusalem, and in all Judea and Samaria, and to the ends of the earth." As someone fully surrendered to God, I am going to live the life of a missionary, whether he ever calls me to a foreign country, or I can't even travel beyond my front door.

For many years, I used work to form my identity. I worked in self-effort, apart from my purpose in Christ. It wasn't until my battle with anxiety that I learned what it meant to lay down working in my own effort and live with God's purpose—doing the better work of the Father. When we know who we are and whose we are, we become strong to do the work of the kingdom and to not fall into Satan's snares.

We are not called to worship our work or the paycheck it brings, but rather our heavenly Father. Our work is meant to reflect God's presence in our lives to all who see us. When we forget this and begin to complain about the difficult parts of our work, we can lose sight of our overall purpose.

God's command to Adam was to rule over and subdue the earth. He asked him to master the animals and assigned him to be a good steward of what God had entrusted to him in the garden. As Adam worked to accomplish these things, he brought glory and honor to God. All his work was an act of both obedience and worship.

Whether your work situation is good, mediocre, or even toxic, God can use you to shine into that environment. It all depends on your perspective. You can be a light to all those you meet as you work for Christ. As Christians, we have the Holy Spirit dwelling inside us, and the darker the room, the easier it is to see the difference when the Spirit's light is shining.

Not only this, but the work we are asked to do can redeem the brokenness of life. You may be stuck in a cubicle for eight hours a day, feeling like you are making no impact for the kingdom. But you can redeem this time by being an example for Christ at your workplace. You can shift your perspective from one of just getting a job done to how can I best help others today? If you are in a job you hate, you can shift your perspective from, "I hate my job," to asking God, "How do you want to use me today?" All it takes to achieve the redemption God wants to do through you for his kingdom is a change of perspective.

REDEEMING YOUR TIME

When we surrender our profession as our top priority and put God first, God provides the money we need and also increases the quality of our lives as we have more time to devote to things that matter most.

Since I work for myself, one of the ways I have made better use of my time is by reshuffling my obligations and making good use of my day. By choosing a schedule, I am more conscious of little time wasters that rob me of using my time in the most efficient way possible. I now use an adapted version of the Jewish model schedule, which means I limit my work hours to six o'clock in the morning to six o'clock in the evening and finish my twelve-hour day knowing I have gotten as much done as I can.

This form of schedule has changed my life. I wake up at 6:30 a.m. and exercise. This leaves me time to spend time in prayer and Bible reading in the morning. I eat, shower, and get to work. I have dinners prepared by six o'clock so I can enjoy the evening. I've also learned to turn off the TV between 5:30–6:30 p.m. to have meaningful conversations with my husband. Granted, I have teenagers, so completing work is not always possible by my six o'clock deadline. In those instances, I move my workday wrap-up to seven or eight o'clock.

What if we used a schedule like this to redeem our work as an act of worship and add life back into our years? How much more physically and spiritually productive we would be!

If you set your own schedule, ask God how you could do all your work, including cleaning and chores, early enough in the day to leave the evenings for cultivating relationships in your life. If you have a set work schedule, could you ask God to help you find ways to do weekly chores during the week to free up the weekends for rest and relationship building?

When we develop better time management, we make more room in our lives for the relationships that not only enrich other's lives but enrich ours as well.

Laying It Down

1. Do you see your work differently because of reading this chapter? Why or why not?

2. In what aspects of your work can you see it as an opportunity to make an impact for God's kingdom?

3. In what ways has your perspective shifted regarding making the most effective use of the time you have?

CHAPTER EIGHTEEN—SURRENDER YOUR POSSESSIONS

It was one of *those* days.

I entered my daughter's room to open her window and slipped on a book on the floor. After having reminded my daughter several times about cleaning her room and taking care of her things, I had had enough. In a fit of frustration, I grabbed a nearby roll of garbage bags and shoved broken pieces of toys, dirty clothes, and dusty stuffed animals into them. After two hours of cleaning, her plush beige rug finally emerged from underneath her endless piles of toys and stuffed animals. Admiring my work, one thought came to my mind:

Where did all this stuff come from?

As Americans, we accumulate a lot of stuff. Before we even realize it, our closets are packed with once-desired articles of clothing, now tossed in a heap on the floor. Uneaten food gets shoved in the back of our cabinets to make room for the new food we have purchased.

Perhaps this is what Jesus means when he says, "Do not store up for yourselves treasures on earth, where moths and vermin destroy, and where thieves break in and steal. But store up for yourselves treasures in heaven, where moths and vermin do not destroy, and where thieves do not break in and steal. For where your treasure is, there your heart will be also" (Matthew 6:19–21). The things we eagerly desire today can end up in our trash cans the next day. God wants us to live lives of simplicity and doesn't want us bogged down in stuff that will keep us bound in debt and enslaved to "keeping up with the Joneses."

Possessions, like anything gone unchecked, can define us. We can use items such as designer shoes, jewelry, or fancy cars as status symbols that cause us to assume an attitude of superiority Christ never wanted us to have. He made himself like the least so he could give God glory, and so should we.

Lay Down Your Treasures

No one loves a good yard sale more than me. One of my favorite pastimes is getting a cup of coffee with my husband then setting out early on a Saturday morning to different towns for what we call "hunting for treasures."

I liken it to a fisherman excited to catch that big fish. All the fisher's hard work gets rewarded when he feels that tug and pulls it in. Not only does he get a feeling of pride as he takes photos of his big catch, but he gets a free dinner too! But the difference between me and a fisherman is he consumes what he catches. Too many of my treasures either get used for a while then forgotten or not used at all and tossed in the garage, only to be at the top of the bag full of items I donate to the local thrift shop. While I'll probably not stop going to yard sales, I can live a life of surrender, even with my favorite hobby.

Pick Up Valuables

It's OK to have possessions if those possessions don't possess you. Jesus didn't want his disciples to rely on possessions when he sent out his disciples in Luke 9:1–6:

> When Jesus had called the Twelve together, he gave them power and authority to drive out all demons and to cure diseases and he sent them out to proclaim the kingdom of God and to heal the sick. He told them: "Take nothing for the journey—no staff, no bag, no bread, no money, no extra shirt. Whatever house you enter, stay there until you leave that town. If people do not welcome you, leave their town and shake the dust off your feet as a testimony against them." So they set out and went from village to village, proclaiming the good news and healing people everywhere.

Similarly, Jesus said, "Foxes have dens and birds have nests, but the Son of Man has no place to lay his head" (Mathew 8:20). Jesus is not against homes or having basic needs met. After all, God loves to lavish good gifts on his children: "If you, then, though you are evil, know how to give good gifts to your children, how much more will your Father in heaven give good gifts to those who ask him!" (Matthew 7:11). And don't forget our homes in heaven! But Jesus didn't have a home on earth because he didn't want to become bogged down with anything that might keep him from accomplishing his Father's work. If any of your possessions are weighing you down, ask God to reveal anything you may have to get rid of to make room for him.

Consider the things you own. Which are items valuable to you, and which items are just stuff? Be intentional about your possessions. Are there items you have that you could do without? Ask yourself before you buy, "Do I *really* need this?" Do you have a ridiculous amount of any particular category of items—clothes, books, shoes? Ask yourself the tough question: do you really need all your stuff?

EMBRACE MINIMALISM

Many of us find God asks us to surrender what we own to find the freedom he wants us to have for his kingdom work. Do you recognize the need to tame your stuff before it conquers you? Here are some tips to help you simplify your life, and help you enjoy what you have:

Collect items you no longer use or need. Go through each closet and get rid of items you have not used in a while (more than six months). Make it a goal to go through one closet or room regularly (once a week).

Have a yard sale. Find a place to store items that aren't just trash and celebrate when you have a large collection by hosting a yard sale and getting paid for your hard work!

Donate. Find a local or web-based charity to bless with your extra possessions. Most local areas have thrift stores that use the proceeds to fund charity work. You might include your children in researching a worthy group and helping deliver items.

Consume your consumables. Try to use all your existing perishable and nonperishable food items before making another trip to the grocery store. You'll be amazed not only at how long you can live off the items you already have but how much money is left in your wallet at the end of the week as well.

Create a Craigslist-style bulletin board. Most churches have bulletin boards that adorn their main entryway or gathering place. Why not post a list of needs and a place for items available to meet those needs? This is a great way to match people's needs with other people's unwanted items. What a great way to help those in need and clean out your home at the same time.

When you stop to think about it, you may feel overwhelmed by the amount of clutter weighing you down in your home. But with God—and perhaps some good friends' help—you can get rid of the clutter for good. Surrender your stuff and keep only the things you need or use on a regular basis.

LAYING IT DOWN

1. Why do you think Jesus didn't want his disciples to carry any necessities with them when he sent them out in Luke 9?

2. Do you feel you own your possessions, or your possessions own you? Why?

3. Besides the tips listed in this chapter, what other ways can you surrender your stuff?

CHAPTER NINETEEN—LIVE A SURRENDERED LIFE

Now that we have taken this journey together toward a life of surrender and analyzed areas where surrender might be the most difficult, let's look at this new surrendered life through the life of Peter. Peter was a man who failed a lot, but with Jesus, there is always redemption. Let's consider a passage in Scripture often talked about or preached in a sermon—John 21:15–19:

> When they had finished eating, Jesus said to Simon Peter, "Simon son of John, do you love me more than these?" "Yes, Lord," he said, "you know that I love you." Jesus said, "Feed my lambs." Again, Jesus said, "Simon son of John, do you love me?" He answered, "Yes, Lord, you know that I love you." Jesus said, "Take care of my sheep." The third time he said to him, "Simon son of John, do you love me?" Peter was hurt because Jesus asked him the third time, "Do you love me?" He said, "Lord, you know all things; you know that I love you." Jesus said, "Feed my sheep. Very truly I tell you, when you were younger you dressed yourself and went where you wanted; but when you are old you will stretch out your hands, and someone else will dress you and lead you where you do not want to go." Jesus said this to indicate the kind of death by which Peter would glorify God. Then he said to him, "Follow me!"

On the morning Jesus was on trial, Peter wept bitterly once he realized what he had done to Jesus. He must have felt a bit like how I felt with my anxiety—alone, downtrodden, and at the end of himself. But his story didn't end there. He got a second chance with Jesus. And we all do! Jesus not only reinstates him to fellowship but also elevates him to be the head of his church. Imagine that—a person who is saved from his brokenness and moved to a place of leadership, all because of an encounter with Jesus.

Living a life of surrender takes sacrifice, hard work, and perseverance. To change old habits of control, independence, and fear to a life where God is in control is bound to result in some mistakes from time to time. But with Jesus, there is a chance to experience his mercy!

Surrender can take us to places of utter desperation. But when we cling to Jesus, we become more Christlike in the process. I'd love to connect with you and hear your stories about how this book has changed your life. Feel free to connect with me on my website, Facebook, or other social media platforms. Let's encourage each other and spur one another on toward love, good deeds—and surrender!

ENDNOTES

Introduction
1. *Merriam-Webster Dictionary,* s.v. "surrender," accessed June 2019, www.merriam-webster.com.
2. *Merriam-Webster,* s.v. "surrender."

Chapter Two
Ginny De Brandt, email to author, May 2021.

Chapter Four
1. Michelle Bengston, *Breaking Anxiety's Grip: How to Reclaim the Peace God Promises.* (Revell: Grand Rapids: 2019), 22.

Chapter Five
1. Erica Wiggenhorn, *Letting God Be Enough: How Striving Keeps You Stuck and How Surrender Sets You Free* (Moody: Chicago; 2021), 8.
2. Kristine Brown, email to author, May 2021.

Chapter Seven
1. *Merriam-Webster Dictionary,* s.v. "pseudo-productivity," accessed June 2019.

Chapter Nine
1. Merriam-Webster Dictionary, s.v. "humility" accessed June 2019.
2. Michelle S. Lazurek, *Righteous and Lost* (Leafwood: Texas, 2017).

Chapter Thirteen

1. Lysa Terkeurst, *Forgiving What You Can't Forget* (Thomas Nelson: Tennessee, 2020), 18.

Chapter Fourteen

1. Melanie Coleman, email to author, May 2021.
2. Nancy Anderson, email to author, May 2021.

Chapter Sixteen

1. Meg Walck, email to author, May 2021.
2. Deborah Coty, email to author, May 2021.

Chapter Seventeen

1. Judy Douglass, email to author, May 2021.

ADDITIONAL RESOURCES

Books

Glynnis Whitwer, *Taming the To-Do List: Choosing Your Best Work Everyday* (Revell: Tennessee, 2015).

Dr. Henry Cloud and Dr. John Townsend, *How People Grow: What the Bible Reveals about Personal Growth* (Grand Rapids: Zondervan, 2004).

Shawn Lovejoy, *The Measure of Our Success* (Grand Rapids: Baker Books, 2012).

Lysa Terkeurst, *It's Not Supposed to Be This Way: Finding Unexpected Strengths When Life's Disappointments Leave You Shattered* (Grand Rapids: Zondervan, 2018).

Susan Scott, *Fierce Conversations.* (New York: American Library Publishers, 2004).

Gary Thomas, *Sacred Marriage: What if God Designed Marriage to Make Us Holy More Than to Make Us Happy?* (Grand Rapids: Zondervan: 2015).

Randy Frazee, *Making Room for Life: Trading Chaotic Lifestyles for Connected Relationships* (Grand Rapids: Michigan, 2003).

Organizations/Websites

Don't have a good local place to donate? The following are worthy organizations to consider blessing with your excess possessions.

- www.dressforsuccess.org allows you to donate dresses, suit jackets, and business suits for disadvantaged women to use during a job interview.
- Your used books and school supplies can supply underprivileged children www.booksforafrica.org.
- www.childsplaycharity.org fills bags full of new toys and games to entertain sick children during their long hospital stay.
- For more ideas, check out http://www.familycircle.com/family-fun/money/donate-items-to-charity/.

ABOUT THE AUTHOR

MICHELLE S. LAZUREK is an award-winning author, speaker, pastor's wife and mother. Winner of the Golden Scroll Children's Book of the Year, the Enduring Light Silver Medal and the Maxwell Award, she is a member of the Christian Author's Network and the Advanced Writers and Speakers Association. She is also an associate literary agent with WordWise Media Services. For more information, please visit her website at michellelazurek.com.

www.ingramcontent.com/pod-product-compliance
Ingram Content Group UK Ltd.
Pitfield, Milton Keynes, MK11 3LW, UK
UKHW021311180426
11947UKWH00015B/1161